Abraham
and his seed

William Henry,

Michael Penny,

Sylvia Penny

ISBN: 978-1-78364-436-0

THE OPEN BIBLE TRUST
Fordland Mount, Upper Basildon,
Reading, RG8 8LU, UK.

www.obt.org.uk

Unless indicated otherwise Scripture quotations are taken from the Holy
Bible, New International Version Anglicised Copyright © 1979, 1984, 2011
Biblica. Used by permission of Hodder & Stoughton Ltd, an Hachette UK
company. All rights reserved. 'NIV' is a registered trademark of Biblica UK
trademark number 1448790.

Publications of The Open Bible Trust must be in accordance with its
evangelical, fundamental and dispensational basis. However, beyond this
minimum, writers are free to express whatever beliefs they may have as
their own understanding, provided that the aim in so doing is to further
the object of The Open Bible Trust. A copy of the doctrinal basis is
available on **www.obt.org.uk** or from:

THE OPEN BIBLE TRUST
Fordland Mount, Upper Basildon,
Reading, RG8 8LU, UK.

Abraham and his seed

Contents

About the authors

William Henry was born in Glasgow in 1949. He qualified as a Chartered Accountant and worked in the accountancy profession for a number of years before moving into academia. At present he is working as an education consultant. He lives in Giffnock with his wife and two daughters.

He has written *The Trinity in* John and has written a number of books with Michael Penny inlcuding *Following Philippians* and *The Will of God: Past and Present.*

Sylvia Penny was born in Bexleyheath, Kent, in 1956. She was educated at Basingstoke High School and Queen Mary's College, before studying accountancy at Oxford Polytechnic. She qualified as a Chartered Accountant and practised in the profession for a number of years, until she went to live in the USA with her husband and was a pastor's wife, taking an active role in the church. On returning to Britain she went back to the accountancy profession.

Other publications by Sylvia Penny include the books *Salvation: Safe and Secure, Satan through the Bible, Introducing God's Plan* (written with Michael Penny) and *Woman to Woman*, a collection of articles for women by women, which she collated and edited.

Michael Penny was born in Ebbw Vale, Gwent, Wales in 1943. He read Mathematics at the University of Reading. He has been Director of Mathematics and Business Studies at Queen Mary's College, Pastor of Grace Church in New Berlin (Wisconsin, USA) and at present is editor and administrator of the Open Bible Trust. He has written several books including *The Bible – Myth or Message?, Approaching the Bible, 40 Problem Passages, Paul – A Mission of Genius, Peter – His life and Letters*

Details of the books mentioned on this page can be seen on the website of The Open Bible Trust. Please visit …

www.obt.org.uk

Chapter 1
Introduction

The importance of Abraham

Abraham is a major figure in all three of the main monotheistic religions – Islam, Judaism and Christianity. Along with Moses and David, he is one of the most frequently mentioned individuals in both the Old and New Testaments. He is regarded as a supreme example of faith in action – particularly as evidenced by his willingness to obey the Lord's command to sacrifice his son, Isaac.

So who was Abraham? He was living in Ur of the Chaldeans around 2,000 BC when God first spoke to him, telling him to leave his family and go to a land that He would show him. Initially Abraham moved (with his family) to Haran, in modern day Turkey, but eventually he left that city and became a tent-dweller as he journeyed to Canaan. The Lord formed a covenant (a binding agreement or contract) with Abraham that contained a threefold promise: that he would be given a land; that he would become a great nation; and that God would bless him and bless all the nations of the earth through him.

During Abraham's long journey, the Lord appeared to him on nine separate occasions, repeating the promises made to him and helping him to grow in his trust of Him. By the end of his life, however, he had not received what had been promised. But the promises were repeated to his son, Isaac and his grandson, Jacob (who later had his name changed to Israel) and to their descendants.

The importance of covenants

The original threefold covenant promise made to Abraham was supplemented by a further covenant with the people of Israel, when the Lord gave Moses the Law as a more detailed expression of His will for His people. An additional covenant was established with David and the Lord promised that He would raise up someone from David's line to sit on his throne and establish a kingdom that would never end. Sadly, the implementation of these promises was delayed by Israel's repeated failure to follow the Lord wholeheartedly. But Jeremiah, in his prophecy, reveals the promise of a New Covenant that the Lord will eventually implement with Israel, through which He would write His Laws on their hearts by His Spirit.

So, by the time we reach the end of the Old Testament we find the nation of Israel back from exile in their land still waiting for the fulfilment of these promises. They were living in the land and they were a nation of considerable size, but they still did not have the influence that the original promise to Abraham had envisaged. Also, they were still waiting for their Messiah, the promised Ruler who would re-establish the kingdom of David His father.

When the Lord Jesus came to them, claiming to be the Messiah, the Son of David, He declared to the disciples that the cup of wine at the feast of Passover was "the new covenant in my blood" (Luke 22:20). But the Jewish leaders failed to recognise His true identity and had Him crucified.

The seed of Abraham

But who were the 'seed of Abraham'? The Jewish people were proud of their pedigree as Abraham's physical descendants and considered themselves to be in a special relationship with God simply because of this. But the Lord Jesus and Paul taught that not all the natural descendants of Abraham were his true seed and other people who had no biological connection with Abraham were to be included in that group. The criterion for membership was whether or not they believed in the Lord Jesus Christ.

So, 2,000 years later, is that still the position? Are all Christians in the church of the twenty-first century the seed of Abraham? Many Christians today believe that that is the case and that the Holy Spirit indwelling Christian believers is an indication that the New Covenant has been implemented through the death and resurrection of Christ.

However, if we follow the development of the Acts Period church, we find at the end of Acts a declaration by Paul that Israel - the seed of Abraham – were now under God's judgment for their failure to accept their Messiah, the Lord Jesus. As a result of this judgment, God's salvation was to be sent to the Gentiles. A few short years after this pronouncement, the Romans destroyed Jerusalem, the survivors of the people of Israel were scattered and Israel ceased to be a nation – a situation that persisted right up to the end of the Second World War.

A change in emphasis?

When we read Paul's letters written after the end of Acts, we find a change in emphasis: there is minimal reference to Abraham or his seed. Instead, Paul speaks about a "mystery" that had been hidden from all previous generations, but which was now being brought to light through a special revelation that Paul and some of his colleagues had received. This mystery concerned a purpose which had been in the mind of God since before creation, to create the church which is the Body of Christ, with Him as its Head. In this church there is no distinction between Jew and Gentile. Individuals are brought into membership of this group solely by their faith in Christ. They are blessed directly by the Lord, not through their link – physical or spiritual – with Abraham.

This book examines the place of Abraham and his seed in Scripture. The early chapters deal with the factual information about Abraham – who he was and the history of his encounters with the Lord. It then moves on to trace the references to Abraham and his seed throughout the Old Testament before going on to discuss the Lord's teaching on Abraham and his seed in the Gospels. Following the Lord's ascension, the Acts of the Apostles describes the growth of the early church of that period and we suggest that Acts, together with the epistles written during that time, show that the seed of Abraham were still very much at the centre of the Lord's purposes. Finally, we explore the situation revealed in Paul's later letters concerning the mystery hidden from previous ages in relation to the church which is the Body of Christ.

Chapter 2

Abraham: The Man

The first time we encounter Abraham is in Genesis 11 when he was still called Abram. There we read:

> This is the account of Terah. Terah became the father of Abram, Nahor and Haran. And Haran became the father of Lot. While his father Terah was still alive, Haran died in Ur of the Chaldeans, in the land of his birth. Abram and Nahor both married. The name of Abram's wife was Sarai, and the name of Nahor's wife was Milcah; she was the daughter of Haran, the father of both Milcah and Iscah. Now Sarai was barren; she had no children.
>
> Terah took his son Abram, his grandson Lot son of Haran, and his daughter-in-law Sarai, the wife of his son Abram, and together they set out from Ur of the Chaldeans to go to Canaan. But when they came to Haran, they settled there. Terah lived 205 years, and he died in Haran. (Genesis 11:27-32)

Here we are introduced to a number of people including Abraham's wife, Sarai (later to be changed to Sarah) and we are told that she was barren. We also learn of Abraham's nephew Lot whose father had died. However, we are given further information about this family at the end of Joshua.

> Joshua said to all the people, "This is what the LORD, the God of Israel, says: 'Long ago your forefathers, including Terah the father of Abraham and Nahor, lived beyond the River *and worshipped other gods*. But I took your father Abraham from the land beyond the River and led him throughout Canaan and gave him many descendants. I gave him Isaac.'" (Joshua 24:2-3)

We see this family were common idolaters from Ur of the Chaldeans, and it was while Abraham was still living there that God first spoke to him (Acts 7:2-4).

Ur was a great city which had been once ruled by Hammurabi, a progressive ruler who had his laws (known as the Code of Hammurabi) carved and displayed on stone pillars, displayed in public so his citizens would know the laws of the land. (The photograph is of one such pillar on display in the Louvre in Paris.)

Faithful Abraham

One may wonder why God chose and spoke to an idolater. However, as we read through Genesis we find that Abraham was a good, law-abiding citizen. He and his family continued to abide by the Code of Hammurabi, the only 'light' he had at that time to follow. For example: in Genesis 15:3 Abraham said to God:

> "You have given me no children; so a servant in my household will be my heir."

This was exactly what Law 191 of the Code of Hammurabi stated. If a wealthy person died without a son and heir (daughters and in-laws could not inherit), then the estate passed to the chief, male steward.

Then, again, we read that Sarah said to Abraham:

> "The LORD has kept me from having children. Go, sleep with my maidservant; perhaps I can build a family through her." (Genesis 16:2)

And we read that Abraham agreed to do it. Again, this was what Law 146 of the Code of Hammurabi permitted. This was not the case of the husband 'taking' the maidservant, but of the wife 'giving' the maidservant to the husband, and any child that the maidservant had would be counted as the child of the master and mistress.

We also find Abraham making 'legal' covenants (or treaties) with neighbours Mamre, Eschol and Aner and becoming allied with them (Genesis 14:13), and also with Abimelech in relation to the well at Beersheba (Genesis 21:27,32).

These things indicate that Abraham tried to live a good life in the light of the Code of Hammurabi, and in that case it is not surprising to read what the Lord said of him.

> "For I have chosen him [Abraham], so that he will direct his children and his household after him to keep the way of the LORD by doing what is right and just." (Genesis 18:19)

If Abraham had lived by and directed his family by the Code of Hammurabi, then God had confidence that Abraham would direct his family and people in the ways of the Lord, and that he would do what is 'right and just'. And we can see this sense of justice in Abraham as he pleaded for Sodom. He started off by saying to the Lord:

> "Will you sweep away the righteous with the wicked? What if there are fifty righteous people in the city? Will you really sweep it away and not spare the place for the sake of the fifty righteous people in it? Far be it from you to do such a thing - to kill the righteous with the wicked, treating the righteous and the wicked alike. Far be it from you! Will not the Judge of all the earth do right?" (Genesis 18:23-25)

The Lord agreed to Abraham's request and Abraham slowly lowered the limit from 50 to 45, and then from 45 to 40 ... and then to 30 ... 20, and finally to 10.

We see his caring character as he was caught between Sarah and Ishmael, the son he had by Hagar (Sarah's handmaiden). We read:

> But Sarah saw that the son whom Hagar the Egyptian had borne to Abraham was mocking, and she said to Abraham, "Get rid of that slave woman and her son, for that slave woman's son will never share in the inheritance with my son Isaac." The matter distressed Abraham greatly because it concerned his son. (Genesis 21:9-11)

Earlier he had also shown great concern for another part of his family, Lot. His nephew, and all his possessions (plus many from Sodom, Gomorrah, Admah, Zeboiim and Bela), had been defeated and carried off by the four kings of Genesis 14:8-12. Abraham's response was to call out all the trained men he had (plus those of Mamre, Eschol and Aner with whom he had an alliance) and pursue the four kings. He defeated them and recovered Lot and his possessions, and all the people who had been captured (Genesis 14:15-16). The king of Sodom was so pleased that he said to Abraham, "Give me the people and keep the goods for yourself"

(Genesis 14:21) but, because of an oath Abraham had made with God, he refused to take anything for himself.

Once more, we can see why God had confidence that Abraham would direct his family and people in the ways of the Lord by doing what is 'right and just'. However, although being faithful to the Code of Hammurabi, and to his family, and to the oath he had taken, he, like us all, was flawed.

Flawed Abraham

In Genesis 12:1 we read that the Lord had told Abraham, "Leave your country, your people and your father's household and go to the land I will show you." However, there was only 'half-obedience'. He did leave his country, but went with Terah (his father) and Lot.

After his father died, the Lord again spoke to Abraham. He left Haran and journeyed on to the land but, again, only 'half-obeyed' as he took Lot with him. In the end it was circumstances which made him 'fully obey'. Genesis 13:7-10 records that "quarrelling arose between Abraham's herdsmen and the herdsmen of Lot" which resulted in Abraham suggesting to Lot that they part company, which they did.

'Half-obedience' was followed by 'half-lies' to both Pharaoh (Genesis 12:13) and Abimelech (Genesis 20:2). He did not tell either that Sarah was his wife. Rather he told them that she was his sister – she was, in fact, his step-sister.

He also seems to have only 'half-understood' the promise that "a son coming from your own body will be your heir" (Genesis 15:4). He appears not to have realised that this would involve Sarah, also. He and his wife were considered to be one flesh (Genesis 2:24), and going with Hagar was not the fulfilment of the Lord's promise (Genesis 16:1-4).

In Genesis 17 the Lord told Abraham that He would "greatly increase your numbers" (verse 2) and as a sign changed his name from *Abram* (which means 'exalted father') to *Abraham* (which means 'father of many'; verse 5). Then, when the Lord clearly stated that the heir would come from Sarah, Abraham appears to have only 'half-believed' it. His reaction was to fall face down, laugh, and say, "If only Ishmael might live under your blessing" (Genesis 17:15-18).

Also, it appears as if Abraham did not tell Sarah about this promise until sometime later, when the Lord returned again and stated, "I will surely return to you about this time next year, and Sarah your wife will have a son", Sarah's reaction was also to laugh in unbelief (Genesis 18:9-12).

Thus in many ways Abraham was faithful, but he was also flawed.

Abraham's growing understanding of God

As we progress from Genesis 12, we see Abraham using different titles of God which, probably, reflect his growing understanding of God. The name that is generally used of God throughout Genesis is *Jehovah* (*Yahweh*), translated "The LORD". However, in Genesis 14 Abraham encounters Melchizedek, who is called the priest of "God Most High, Creator of Heaven and Earth" (Genesis 14:18-20). A few verses later, when Abraham refused to accept any share of the spoils of battle, when he and the king of Sodom had defeated Kedorlaomer and the kings allied with him, Abraham himself refers to God as "The Lord, God Most High, Creator of heaven and earth" (Genesis 14:22) – the same title used by Melchizedek.

Then, at the start of chapter 15, when God appears to him in a vision, Abraham addresses Him as "Sovereign Lord" (Genesis 15:2) and in this vision God confirmed to Abraham that he will have a son from his own body and that his offspring will be like the stars in the sky. The Lord also predicted the suffering of Abraham's descendants in Egypt and their ultimate deliverance.

In Genesis 17:1, when Abraham is 99, the Lord introduces Himself to Abraham as "God Almighty" (*El Shaddai*), a name which should have re-enforced Abraham's faith in God's ability to deliver the promise that he and Sarah would have a son and many descendants.

Abraham and Isaac

Having been told that Sarah would have a child within a year, Abraham moved into the region of the Negev, and there Abraham 'half-lied' about Sarah being his sister to King Abimelech, who took her from him (Genesis 20:1-2). Now in Genesis 17:17 we read that Sarah was about 90 years old, and so what was a king doing wanting to take an elderly woman into his harem? We may ask a similar question about Pharaoh some 30 years or so earlier (Genesis 12:15). Although about 60, when Pharaoh's officials saw Sarah "they praised her to Pharaoh" and she was taken into his harem.

So did Sarah simply not age in physical appearance? Or did God start an external rejuvenation of Sarah many years before she was to have a child? Later, when Israel was in the wilderness we read that during their forty years of wandering in the wilderness neither the clothes nor the sandals of the Israelites wore out (Deuteronomy 29:5). Was Sarah also preserved 'externally' in some miraculous way? We may never know, but the 'internal' rejuvenation took place when she was over 90. She became pregnant by Abraham, gave birth to a son, and called him Isaac, which means 'laughter'.

However, some years after this promised child had been born, God told Abraham:

> "Take your son, your only son, Isaac, whom you love, and go to the region of Moriah. Sacrifice him there as a burnt offering on one of the mountains I will tell you about." (Genesis 22:2)

We do not know how Abraham may have felt. We are simply told:

> Early the next morning Abraham got up and saddled his donkey. He took with him two of his servants and his son Isaac. When he

had cut enough wood for the burnt offering, he set out for the place God had told him about. (Genesis 22:3)

And then in the next verse we have what appears to be either a remarkable statement, or one of wishful thinking. After three days of travel, Abraham said to his two servants:

> "Stay here with the donkey while I and the boy go over there. *We* will worship and then *we* will come back to you."

From what we read elsewhere in the Bible, this appears to have been a very genuine statement on the part of Abraham. In Hebrews 11:17-19 we read:

> By faith Abraham, when God tested him, offered Isaac as a sacrifice. He who had received the promises was about to sacrifice his one and only son, even though God had said to him, "It is through Isaac that your offspring will be reckoned." Abraham reasoned that God could raise the dead, and figuratively speaking, he did receive Isaac back from death.

Abraham had seen Sarah rejuvenated; her dead womb brought back to life. We can only imagine the great effect that must have had on Abraham's faith in God. Paul comments on this in Romans.

> As it is written: "I have made you a father of many nations." He is our father in the sight of God, in whom he believed - the God who gives life to the dead and calls things that are not as though they were. Against all hope, Abraham in hope believed and so became the father of many nations, just as it had been said to him, "So shall your offspring be." Without weakening in his faith, he faced the fact that his body was as good as dead - since he was about a hundred years old - and that Sarah's womb was also dead. Yet he did not waver through unbelief regarding the promise of God, but was strengthened in his faith and gave glory to God,

being fully persuaded that God had power to do what he had promised. (Romans 4:17-21)

Here we read about Sarah's womb being dead. Here we read not only that Abraham believed in God, but he believed in the God "who gives life to the dead". So Abraham reasoned that if God had promised that it was through Isaac that his posterity would be as the stars in the sky, and that as God had brought Sarah's dead womb back to life, then God would have to, and would be capable of, bringing Isaac back to life. He was fully persuaded that God had the power to do what He had promised. God promised that it was through Isaac, therefore it would be through Isaac. So, if Isaac was dead, God would have to bring him back to life! What logic! And what faith!!

Abraham may have been flawed, but he eventually reached the place where God wanted him to be. It took him a long time to understand God's promises to him, but he eventually did so.

It took him ages to believe the purpose God had for him through a promised child he and Sarah would have, but he eventually did so. It took him years to fully obey the initial command to leave his home and family but ... he immediately obeyed the command to sacrifice Isaac. Then, at that point, his faith was mature, and his faithfulness was made evident to all by his willingness to obey.

Abraham the Prophet

Sarah's death is recorded in Genesis 23 and Abraham's in Genesis 25. There is much more recorded in Genesis about Abraham, but clearly we do not have a fully detailed account of all his life. However, in Genesis 20:7 he is called a 'prophet' and, as a prophet, he foresaw two significant events in the far future. We are told about these in the New Testament, but we read nothing about them in Genesis.

Our Lord Jesus Christ said of him:

"Your father Abraham rejoiced at the thought of seeing my day; he saw it and was glad." (John 8:56)

So he saw Christ's day and he also saw beyond that; he 'saw' the heavenly Jerusalem.

> By faith he made his home in the promised land like a stranger in a foreign country; he lived in tents, as did Isaac and Jacob, who were heirs with him of the same promise. For he was looking forward to the city with foundations, whose architect and builder is God. (Hebrews 11:9-10; see also Hebrews 11:14-18 and 12:22)

It would seem that this vision of the heavenly city may have been given to Abraham when he was first called by God, when he was still living in Ur of the Chaldeans. However, we have no idea as to when he was given any information about Christ's day. None-the-less such visions, together with the experiences he went through, must have helped him, shaped him, and inspired him to be the great man of faith that he became. Flawed? Yes, for all have sinned and fall short of the glory of God (Romans 3:23). Faithful? Yes, and the rocky journey of his life is a great inspiration to us to be faithful in our walk also.

> Yet he [Abraham] did not waver through unbelief regarding the promise of God, but was strengthened in his faith and gave glory to God, being fully persuaded that God had power to do what he had promised. This is why "it was credited to him as righteousness."
>
> The words "it was credited to him" were written not for him alone, but also for us, to whom God will credit righteousness - for us who believe in him who raised Jesus our Lord from the dead. He was delivered over to death for our sins and was raised to life for our justification. (Romans 4:20-25)

Conclusion

Abraham, although flawed like everyone else, was a man of great faith, and can be an inspiration to us. However, unlike us, he was aided in his walk with God and in the deepening of his faith by several direct encounters with the Lord. The next chapter explores the circumstances of each of these interactions and the ways in which they strengthened his trust in God.

Chapter 3
The Lord's Appearances to Abraham

Introduction

In the 14 chapters in Genesis that deal with the life of Abraham, there are nine occasions when the Lord either spoke to Abraham, appeared to him in a vision, or actually met him face to face. As we go through these, it is worth noting that on every occasion, the Lord either promised something to Abraham, or He confirmed a promise he had already made to him. There are three major promises relating to:

- land,
- his offspring, and
- the blessing they will be to everyone on earth.

Each of these is repeated several times. Also, some of these promises are referred to as "covenants". So, first of all, what is a covenant, and how do we recognise one?

Covenants

Briefly, the basic idea of a covenant in Abraham's time was the uniting in purpose of the people entering into the covenant. Often they were to do with peace treaties, and setting up mutual defences against a common enemy. Also, they were often sealed with an oath. Basically it was a very solemn promise similar to our practice of going to a solicitor to sign a document, such as a will, in front of witnesses. In Abraham's time, though, covenants often involved a ritual, which may have included the sacrifice of an animal which was then divided into two parts, so that the parties to the covenant could walk between the pieces.

The Hebrew word for "making" a covenant literally meant "cutting" a covenant – which is actually very similar to our modern day equivalent of "cutting a deal". So they used to "cut covenants". They used the same word when they talked about cutting off heads and cutting off lives. So, altogether, a covenant involved a cutting, a sacrifice, an oath, a peace agreement, and a unity of purpose between the parties involved. It was certainly recognised as being a very solemn promise.

God's first encounter with Abraham

When was the first encounter between God and Abraham? Interestingly enough, this is not as obvious as one might think. The whole episode is much clearer in the New Testament, in Acts 7, when Stephen gave a long speech just before he was stoned to death. Stephen said:

> The God of glory appeared to our father Abraham *while he was still in Mesopotamia*, before he lived in Haran. "Leave your country and your people," God said, "and go to the land I will show you." So he left the land of the Chaldeans and settled in Haran. After the death of his father, God sent him to this land where you are now living. (Acts 7:2-4)

So, that first encounter, which took place when Abraham was living in Ur of the Chaldeans, involved the promise of a land. But, in fact, the promise was much more wide-ranging.

It is at the beginning of Genesis 12 that we find out what God had said to Abraham while he was still in Mesopotamia:

The Lord had said to Abram, "Leave your country, your people and your father's household and go to the *land* I will show you.

    I will make you into *a great nation* and I will bless you, I will make your name great, and you will be a blessing. I will bless those who bless you, and whoever curses you I will curse, and *all peoples on earth will be blessed through you.*" (Genesis 12:1-3)

Here we have the first great promise made to Abraham by the Lord. It is generally known as the "Abrahamic covenant." It was a solemn promise given by God to Abraham. It involved a "cutting off". Abraham was to cut himself off from his country, his people and his family, and travel to a distant land. In response, God would make him into a great nation, He would bless him, and Abraham would be a blessing, and ultimately all peoples on earth would be blessed through Abraham.

This was a remarkable promise in itself, but even more so because of one little detail included at the end of Genesis 11 which is very easy to gloss over. Verse 30 records, "Now Sarai was barren; she had no children." Right from the beginning Abraham must have questioned how he could be the father of a great nation, when his wife had been unable to have any children. And yet despite this, he obeyed and he went.

It is interesting to speculate whether, on this first occasion, Abraham's faith was reasonable, or whether he just employed what some would call today "blind obedience". Did Abraham have good solid reasons for his faith in what God had promised? Scripture does not tell us that Abraham was given any proof that what God told him would definitely happen. If anything, it seems there was more to the contrary. Sarai was barren, and the land to which he was travelling was far away from the civilised world of Mesopotamia. When he got there he would have to literally set up camp and live in tents, rather than enjoy the comfortable city life he had known up until then.

It's not surprising that Abraham, time and again in Scripture, is praised for his great faith, which, as we know from Hebrews 11:1, is being sure of what we hope for and certain of something that we cannot see.

God's second encounter with Abraham

God's second encounter with Abraham only took place once he had finally arrived in the land of Canaan. Haran, which was half way to Canaan, was not good enough. The Lord had to be *wholly* obeyed.

Genesis 12:5 tells us that he travelled from Haran to Canaan with his nephew Lot, so he did not *quite* leave all his family behind, as he had also been instructed, so he still was not totally obedient at this time.

Once they arrived, they travelled to Shechem, and it was here that the Lord appeared to Abraham a second time. The Lord said to Abraham, "To your offspring *I will give this land*." In his first encounter, although the Lord had told him to go to a land that He would show him, He had not specifically promised this land to him. Here for the first time, He does. At this stage, however, nothing more is said. Abraham is given no details of how large this land would be, how far it would extend, or anything else about it. And although his offspring are mentioned again, no details are given as to when he would start having any children – and at this point Abraham was now 75 years old, and Sarai was 65 years old – not exactly the ages one would expect to begin a family.

God's third encounter with Abraham

After some time, both Abraham and Lot had become so wealthy, and had so many flocks and herds and tents that they could not stay in the same area together. So Abraham told Lot to choose where he would like to settle, and he would then go elsewhere. Lot chose the plain of Jordan as it was well watered and the best land at that time. Unfortunately, it also included Sodom and Gomorrah, but that did not deter Lot, and he went and pitched his tents near Sodom.

Genesis 13:18 tells us Abraham then moved all his tents and possessions to the area of Hebron, which was beyond the hills to the west of the plain of Jordan, well away from where Lot had decided to settle.

It was then, once he had parted company with Lot, that Abraham had his third encounter with the Lord. Leaving only part of his family had not been good enough. The Lord had to be *wholly* obeyed before he had this third encounter.

On this occasion the Lord said to Abraham:

> "Lift up your eyes from where you are and look north and south, east and west. All the land that you see I will give to you and your offspring for ever. I will make your offspring like the dust of the earth, so that if anyone could count the dust, then your offspring could be counted. Go, walk through the length and breadth of the land, for I am giving it to you." (Genesis 13:14-17)

Two of the previous promises were repeated by the Lord during this third encounter. He promised Abraham all the land he could see and He promised him that his offspring would be like the dust of the earth.

God's fourth encounter with Abraham

In Genesis 15 we have a detailed account of the Lord's fourth encounter with Abraham. We are given even more details of God's covenant with him. Again, it is all to do with Abraham's offspring, and the land they would live in. But now, his future offspring are described as countless as the stars of heaven. Previously, they had been described as the dust of the earth. Now, the land promised is going to extend from the river of Egypt (probably the Nile) to the river Euphrates. Previously it had been all the land he could see when he settled in Hebron. So, the descriptions given here are more extensive than those that were given before.

Interestingly, verse 6 tells us that "Abraham believed the Lord, and he credited it to him as righteousness," and yet we see that Abraham was, at the very least, puzzled by the promises made to him. He told God that, as he had no children, a servant in his household would be his heir (almost as if he thought God might not be aware of this!). To be fair to Abraham, by this time about ten years had gone by since God had promised that he would be the father of a great nation, and yet still there was no sign of this happening.

He also asked God how he could definitely know that he would gain possession of all this land (verse 8). Although he believed what God told him, he was still very puzzled as to how it was all going to happen, as on the face of it, none of it looked very likely. So although Abraham is always described as a man of great faith, Scripture does not put him on a pedestal either. He obviously had his doubts, his times of questioning what God had promised, and needed to have it confirmed to him.

In response, God made a solemn covenant with Abraham, and again this involved "a cutting". Abraham was to bring several animals and birds to the Lord, which were to be cut in two and arranged opposite one another. Later a smoking brazier and a blazing torch from the Lord passed between the pieces. As indicated on page 21 above, passing between animals that had been divided in two was how covenants were solemnised in Old Testament times, rather than signing and sealing a document, as we do today. So although this seems rather a peculiar procedure to go through, it would not have been so in Abraham's time. This was a very solemn promise that was certainly going to be kept, and this was the proof of it to Abraham.

It was also an unconditional covenant. We can see that the burden was completely on the Lord's side. Abraham was required to do nothing. Only the Lord passed between the pieces. Abraham did not, and this was unusual, as when covenants were made, usually both parties passed between the pieces. The Lord simply told him what was going to happen. The fact that Abraham believed this, however, was credited to him as righteousness. Thus the concept of "justification by faith" is established very early in Scripture, and Abraham is referred to many times by Paul in the New Testament as an example of this principle. Abraham lived hundreds of years *before* the Law of Moses was given, and so he is a wonderful example to *prove* that righteousness was never given as a result of keeping the Mosaic Law as Abraham was credited with righteousness long before the Law was given.

So, the onus was totally on the Lord to fulfil this covenant. Was it ever completely fulfilled? Certainly Abraham became the father of a great nation, though it is debatable whether his offspring could be described as being as countless as the stars, and as numerous as the dust of the earth.

But - what about the land? Did Israel ever possess the land all the way from the Nile to the Euphrates? Certainly in Solomon's day the land extended the furthest it ever has, but they never conquered as far as the Euphrates. Also, has the nation been a blessing to all people on earth? Was this ever fulfilled? The answer to that is – "not completely". They have been a blessing to some people, but not to all people on earth.

So it seems, at some time in the future, these promises to Abraham have yet to be completely fulfilled. If God keeps to His word, and He will, then we must expect Him to do this.

God's fifth encounter with Abraham

There is then a gap of about 13 or 14 years before the Lord's next three encounters with Abraham – the fifth, sixth and seventh, which all happened in quick succession within the space of one year.

Maybe this gap occurred because it was then that Sarah put her own plan into action, and Abraham agreed to it. Sarah gave her maidservant, Hagar, to Abraham to build a family through her, as Sarah was about 75 years old at this time, and thought she would never have children herself.

The result was Ishmael, who was the father of all the Arabic nations. Abraham was 86 years old when Ishmael was born.

So it was another 13 years later, when Abraham was 99 years old, that he had his fifth encounter with the Lord. This comes in Genesis 17, and here it is very clear that God physically appeared to Abraham. Verse 1 says "the Lord appeared to him" and verse 22 says "When he had finished speaking with Abraham, God went up from him." Apart from when Abraham had first arrived in the land 25 years earlier, the Lord had never since appeared to him face to face. He had spoken to Abraham, and He had come to him in a vision, but here, once again, He appeared to him and talked to him face to face.

God confirmed His covenant with Abraham, but this time He also told him he would be the father of *many* nations. No longer was he to be the father of just one "great nation"; this was now expanded to many nations.

On this occasion He also told him his name was no longer to be Abram, but Abraham. Abram means "exalted father" but Abraham means "father of many".

He also said this was to be an everlasting covenant, and that the whole of the land of Canaan, where Abraham was now an alien, would, in the future, be an everlasting possession for him and his descendants.

As the years had gone by, each time the Lord spoke to Abraham He added a little more to what He had said before. Of course, since the last time He had spoken to Abraham, he had become the father of Ishmael, and so it was clear that Abraham would not only be the father of the Jews, but he would also be father of all Arabic nations coming from Ishmael. And of course, we know that in the course of time, after Sarah died, he also married Keturah, and fathered six more children through her, among them Midian, and so he was also father of the Midianites, among several other nations. So he did eventually become the "father of many nations" as promised by the Lord.

Then, in Genesis 17:9-11, the Lord mentioned circumcision to Abraham for the first time, and this was to be the sign of the everlasting covenant between Himself and Abraham, and with the descendants to come from Abraham. For the first time a condition was added to the covenant. The Lord said:

- Genesis 17:3 "As for me..."
    - I will make you a father of nations.
    - I will change your name to Abraham (father of many).
    - I will make you very fruitful.
    - I will make nations of you, and kings will come from you.
    - I will establish my covenant as an everlasting covenant between me and you and your descendants to be your God and the God of your descendants.
    - I will give them the land of Canaan as an everlasting possession.

- Genesis 17:9 "As for you..."
    - You must keep my covenant – and this specifically means the circumcision of all males.
    - Any uncircumcised male has broken the covenant and is to be cut off from the covenant people (verse 14).

- God finishes in Genesis 17:19 by saying that He will establish his covenant with Isaac and his descendants after him.

Previously it had been unconditional, but now any male descendant who was not circumcised would forfeit the blessing.

> Then God said to Abraham, "As for you, you must keep my covenant, you and your descendants after you for the generations to come. This is my covenant with you and your descendants after you, the covenant you are to keep: Every male among you shall be circumcised. You are to undergo circumcision, and it

will be the sign of the covenant between me and you." (Genesis 17:9-11)

Once again, cutting was involved as a sign of the covenant. The first "cutting" was symbolic, when Abraham cut himself off from his father's house and his land. The second "cutting" was physical, when he offered the animal sacrifices mentioned in Genesis 15, and the Lord passed between the pieces. Here, this third "cutting" was also physical - the act of circumcision - but this time it involved cutting himself. Each time the "cutting" became more personal. Circumcision bore the shame of mutilation, and it prefigured Christ's offering of himself as the ultimate covenant offering, the ultimate shame and "cutting off" on the cross.

Twice in chapter 17 we are told that Abraham fell, face down, in front of the Lord. First, when the Lord told him, again, that He would greatly increase his numbers, and second when He told Abraham specifically that Sarah would be blessed and be the mother of many nations, and that many kings would come from her.

It was only then that God specifically named Sarah as the mother. Previously she had never been mentioned. Maybe this was partly the reason that Sarah had come up with her plan to make God's promise come true through Hagar.

Abraham's reaction at first is total disbelief at this. Genesis 17:17 says:

> Abraham fell face down; he laughed and said to himself, "Will a son be born to a man a hundred years old? Will Sarah bear a child at the age of ninety?"

The fact that the Lord had finally explicitly said that Sarah was to be the mother was obviously beyond his comprehension. He was totally amazed! But he had not taken into account the Lord's decision to make the impossible happen. God replied:

"Yes, but your wife Sarah will bear you a son, and you will call him Isaac. I will establish my covenant with him as an everlasting covenant for his descendants after him." (Genesis 17:19)

So in this fifth encounter between Abraham and the Lord, Abraham learned several new things. He learned that Sarah was definitely to be the mother of the great nation he had been promised, and he learned that he would be the father of not only one great nation, but many. He learned that the son he was going to have with Sarah was to be called Isaac, and he learned that he would be born the very next year. At last the Lord was very precise with the details.

He also stated very clearly that it was through *Isaac* that his everlasting covenant was to be established. Ishmael was to be made into a great nation also, but *not* the covenant nation.

Immediately, that very day, Abraham took Ishmael and all those born in his household or bought with his money and circumcised every single one, in obedience to the Lord's word, and as a sign of this everlasting covenant.

God's sixth encounter with Abraham

Shortly after this comes the sixth encounter between the Lord and Abraham, recorded in Genesis 18. Again, this was an actual physical appearance, rather than just a word or a vision. It is also made clear that the Lord appeared as a man this time, as in Genesis 18:2 we are told that Abraham looked up and saw three men standing nearby. Later we discover two are angels, and one is the Lord.

This time the Lord did not let many years go by. In fact, it seems the main reason for this particular encounter was actually for Sarah's benefit, as the first thing the Lord said to Abraham was, "Where is your wife Sarah?". When he replied that she was in the tent close by, the Lord said, loud enough for Sarah to hear:

"I will surely return to you about this time next year, and Sarah your wife will have a son." (Genesis 18:10)

Sure enough, Sarah was listening at the entrance to the tent, which was behind where the Lord was standing, and when she heard this, her reaction was perfectly understandable. She laughed to herself, and thought:

"After I am worn out and my master is old, will I now have this pleasure?" (Genesis 18:12)

In other words, she could not believe what she had heard! The Lord heard Sarah's thought, and said to Abraham:

"Why did Sarah laugh and say, "Will I really have a child, now that I am old?" Is anything too hard for the Lord? I will return to you at the appointed time next year and Sarah will have a son." (Genesis 18:3-4)

Sarah was afraid, maybe because she realised this man had accurately read her mind, and so she denied laughing. However, the Lord insisted, "Yes, you did laugh." Perhaps this was intended as a sign to her that the One who could read her inner thoughts, could also perform the inner miracle of bringing her dead womb to life. In her hearing, He had asked, "Is anything too hard for the Lord?" The answer was, very clearly, "No!"

Immediately after this, we seem to be side-tracked from the story of Abraham and Sarah, and have a very unusual exchange between Abraham and the Lord, and it is described in some detail at the end of Genesis 18. Briefly, this is the story of Sodom and Gomorrah, and the Lord's intention to destroy them completely, as their sin was so extreme. However, Abraham pleaded with the Lord not to destroy them if he could find just a few righteous people living there. No doubt he had the safety of his nephew, Lot, in mind when he bargained with the Lord. The final result was that just four people escaped the destruction - Lot, his wife, and his two daughters, and all the details of this are given in Genesis 19.

It seems the Lord went out of his way to honour Abraham's request, despite the fact it was obvious that even Lot's family had been tainted by living among the people in Sodom. Lot's wife was so reluctant to leave that she looked back and turned into a pillar of salt.

After the story of Sodom and Gomorrah, Genesis 20 returns to Abraham and Sarah. Here there is the narrative involving Sarah and Abimelech, the king of Gerar. Although Sarah was nearly 90 years old, she was attractive enough to be added to his harem, and we have looked at the possible reasons for this in the previous chapter. Genesis 20 gives us the details of how the Lord intervened, and made sure that Abimelech never touched Sarah. Instead, Abimelech showered Abraham with sheep and cattle and slaves and land to live wherever he liked – all on account of Sarah.

After this Sarah finally became pregnant, and gave birth to Isaac. Abraham was 100 years old, and Sarah was 90. It seems that the Lord had deliberately set out to test both Abraham and Sarah's faith, and, as a result, to strengthen it against all odds.

Eight days after Isaac was born, he was circumcised, and Sarah said:

> "God has brought me laughter, and everyone who hears about this will laugh with me." (Genesis 21:6)

God had literally brought Sarah joy and laughter with the birth of Isaac, and even his very name, Isaac, means "he laughs".

God's seventh encounter with Abraham

The Lord's seventh encounter with Abraham came when he was 100 years old. So it was less than a year after Abraham's bargaining with him over Sodom. This encounter however is a very brief one.

On the day that Isaac was weaned Abraham held a great feast, but Ishmael, who by this time was 14 years old, was mocking, and so Sarah said to Abraham:

> "Get rid of that slave woman and her son, for that slave woman's son will never share in the inheritance with my son Isaac." (Genesis 21:10)

Abraham was distressed by this, as obviously Ishmael and Isaac were both his sons. It was because of Abraham's distress that he had this seventh, brief encounter with the Lord.

The Lord spoke to Abraham, and said:

> "Do not be so distressed about the boy and your maidservant. Listen to whatever Sarah tells you, because it is through Isaac that your offspring will be reckoned. I will make the son of the maidservant into a nation also, because he is your offspring." (Genesis 21:13)

So the Lord soothed Abraham, and reminded him that He had promised to bless Ishmael too, because he was also Abraham's son. However, He also confirmed, once again, that it was through Isaac that the promised nation was to come. And of course, we know ultimately that it was through Isaac that the most important Offspring of all would come – namely the Lord Jesus Christ.

God's eighth encounter with Abraham

God's final two encounters with Abraham were a number of years later. This was when Abraham experienced the most extreme test of his faith, when he was asked by God to sacrifice Isaac. In Genesis 22:2 God said to Abraham:

Take your son, your only son, Isaac, whom you love, and go to the region of Moriah. Sacrifice him there as a burnt offering on one of the mountains I will tell you about.

Here the Lord went out of His way to emphasise the enormity of what He asked Abraham to do. He referred to Isaac as his *only* son, the son whom he loved.

Despite the fact that Abraham knew that God's promise to him was to be fulfilled through Isaac, he went ahead and faithfully prepared to do what God had asked him to do. It is only in the New Testament, in Hebrews 11:19, that we discover *why* Abraham was ready to do the unthinkable. There we are told "Abraham reasoned that God could raise the dead, and figuratively speaking, he did receive Isaac back from death."

This was an amazing piece of reasoning, and an amazing act of faith, as at this time no person had ever been raised from the dead. There was nothing for Abraham to base this on, except his complete faith and confidence in what God had told him.

God's ninth encounter with Abraham

After being asked by the Lord to take Isaac and sacrifice him, Abraham set off to do this early the very next morning. Abraham did not delay in obeying the Lord.

It took him, Isaac and the two servants travelling with them three days to reach the mountain God had chosen, and it was there that Abraham had his ninth (and final) encounter with the Lord. It was only when Abraham had the knife in his hand to slay his son Isaac, that the angel of the Lord called out from heaven, and told him not to lay a hand on him. He said:

> "Do not do anything to him. Now I know that you fear God, because you have not withheld from me your son, your only son." (Genesis 22:12)

Abraham saw a ram caught in a thicket nearby, and so he sacrificed it instead of Isaac. Once the ram had been sacrificed as a burnt offering, the Lord spoke to Abraham for what would be the last time in his life, (even though he lived another 60 to 70 years), and the Lord said to him:

> "I swear by myself … that because you have done this and have not withheld your son, your only son, I will surely bless you and make your descendants as numerous as the stars in the sky and as the sand on the seashore. Your descendants will take possession of the cities of their enemies, and through your offspring all nations on earth will be blessed, because you have obeyed me." (Genesis 22:16-18)

So here we have the culmination of Abraham's faith. In this last encounter with the Lord, it was obvious God was completely satisfied with Abraham. He had passed the ultimate test. He did not withhold the most precious thing to him in the whole world – the son he dearly loved, and whom he had waited for, patiently, for so many years.

Again, the Lord repeated all three of His covenant promises to Abraham, to do with the land, his offspring, and being a blessing to all nations on earth, and once again, as this was a solemn covenant, a "cutting" was involved - and this is the fourth "cutting" - symbolically, the ultimate sacrifice of his only son and heir.

This was the greatest "cutting" of all, and one which prefigured, so perfectly, the sacrifice of our Lord and Saviour Jesus Christ on the cross. Also, as we've seen from the quote in Hebrews 11, this prefigured Christ's resurrection from the dead, as, symbolically, Abraham received Isaac back from the dead.

Conclusion

Abraham had nine encounters with the Lord during his lifetime. And on each occasion one or more of the three great promises made to Abraham were repeated to him, with more and more details being given as the years went by.

He lived his life in faith that the Lord would, one day in the future, fulfil these promises completely. We can see his faith deepened to such an extent that he was prepared to sacrifice Isaac believing that if the Lord was to fulfil his promises he would have to raise Isaac from the dead. Finally Abraham died, at the grand old age of 175 years, never having seen any of these promises fulfilled.

However, the remainder of the Old Testament traces the experiences of his descendants through Isaac and Jacob (Israel). Repeatedly, the Israelites were reminded of the promises made to Abraham and his seed. They are the "golden thread" running through their tortuous journey – physical and spiritual – and it is to this subject that we now turn.

Chapter 4

Abraham and his seed throughout the Old Testament

Introduction

As indicated in the previous chapter, the relationship between the Lord and Abraham was a covenant relationship built around three promises. These were initially introduced to Abraham by the Lord in Genesis 12 and then explained or expanded during the further encounters between them. The three covenant promises related to the provision of a land for Abraham and his descendants together with promises that his seed would be blessed and greatly multiplied and that they would be a blessing to all the other nations on the earth.

The promises as initially stated were unconditional but in Genesis 17 we find the introduction of the practice of circumcision. There were conditions to be met by both the Lord and Abraham.

Many of God's interactions with Abraham were to test and develop His trust and were accompanied by a repetition and expansion of the earlier promises.

The conditional and unconditional elements of the covenant

We read of Abraham's death in Genesis 25, without him having seen much of the fulfilment of God's promises. He had been blessed, because he became very rich, certainly in terms of livestock. But he was still living in a tent so there was no sign of the promise being fulfilled in relation to the land or of him being a blessing to the whole earth. He had eight sons that we know of but that was hardly a great nation.

Nevertheless, the Lord confirmed His threefold promise to Isaac:

> "… to you and your descendants I will give all these lands and will confirm the oath I swore to your father Abraham. I will make your descendants as numerous as the stars in the sky and will give them all these lands, and through your offspring all nations on earth will be blessed, because Abraham obeyed me and kept my requirements, my commandments, my decrees and my laws." (Genesis 26:3-5)

And also to Jacob:

> There above it (the ladder reaching up to heaven) stood the Lord and he said, "I am the Lord, the God of your father Abraham and the God of Isaac. I will give you and your descendants the land on which you are lying. Your descendants will be like the dust of the earth and you will spread out to the west and to the east, to the north and to the south. All peoples on earth will be blessed through you and your offspring." (Genesis 28:13-14)

The same threefold promise was still there. But in the Lord's words to Isaac there is again the suggestion that the enjoyment of these benefits will have a condition attached. In Genesis 17 we find the condition of circumcision. But Abraham's obedience was more far-reaching than just that practice. Genesis 26:5 indicates that Abraham kept all the Lord's requirements.

So, again there is a suggestion that the fulfilment of the covenant promises was dependent upon Abraham's obedience and, by implication, the continuing obedience of Isaac and Jacob and the children of Israel.

How do we make sense of this conditional/unconditional element? It seems strange to make unconditional promises to Abraham and his descendants and then introduce conditions later. It would appear that, although the promise was sure and will one day be fulfilled, the timing of that fulfilment depended upon the obedience of Abraham's descendants. As Burch says:

> We should understand God's covenant with Abraham before this time as unbreakable and everlasting. What God was adding now was the sense of the covenant being renewed between Him and each succeeding generation ... They were to live like Abraham and walk before God as Abraham did. It was to be a continually living covenant. (Glen Burch, *Abraham's Progress in the Covenants of God*, p10)

As we follow the history of Israel throughout the Old Testament, we can see this pattern emerging: when Israel disobeyed the Lord, mainly by following other gods, He punished them by putting them under the heel of oppressing nations, or even by exile. Yet He never forgot them and, when they cried out to Him, He turned from punishing them to bless them. It was their inability to follow the Lord fully that prevented the fulfilment of the promises, but the nation was never abandoned by the Lord.

The Abrahamic covenant can be traced right through the Old Testament.

The Abrahamic covenant in the historical books

As we explore the Old Testament we find repeated references to God's unconditional promise to Abraham, Isaac and Jacob and the Israelites are continually urged to follow His ways as a means of blessing. The Lord is repeatedly identified as the God of Abraham, Isaac and Jacob. For example:

- *In Egypt:* When the Israelites were in bondage in Egypt, the Lord raised up Moses to deliver them because:

  > God remembered his covenant with Abraham, Isaac and Jacob. (Exodus 2:24)

  Moses was instructed to go to the Israelites and inform them that it was the God of their fathers who had sent him to deliver them:

  > God also said to Moses, "Say to the Israelites, 'The Lord, the God of your fathers – the God of Abraham, the God of Isaac and the God of Jacob – has sent me to you.' This is my name forever, the name by which I am to be remembered from generation to generation." (Exodus 3:15)

- *As Moses went to meet Pharaoh*: When the Lord commissioned Moses to go in to Pharaoh to demand Israel's release, He reminded him that He was the Lord who had appeared to Abraham, Isaac and Jacob (Exodus 6:2-3). He added:

  > I also established my covenant with them to give them the land of Canaan, where they lived as aliens. Moreover I have heard the groaning of the Israelites, whom the Egyptians are enslaving, and I have remembered my covenant. (Exodus 6:4-5)

- *After the golden calf incident:* After the people of Israel had made a golden calf to worship, the Lord threatened to destroy them for their sin but Moses pleaded on their behalf. The principal argument he used to persuade God not to destroy Israel was to call to mind the covenant promises. Hearing Moses' argument, the Lord relented and spared Israel. Moses said:

> "Remember your servants, Abraham, Isaac and Israel, to whom you swore by your own self: 'I will make your descendants as numerous as the stars in the sky and I will give your descendants all this land I promised them, and it will be their inheritance forever.'" (Exodus 32:13)

- *When setting out the requirements of the Law:* When the Lord was setting out the detailed requirements for Israel to follow the Law, He warned them not to be disobedient. The Lord set out before them all the punishment He was going to inflict on them, describing in detail the laying waste of the land, the destruction of the people and the exile of the survivors. Then the Lord seemed to pause, and added:

> But if they confess their sins and the sins of their fathers ... then when their uncircumcised hearts are humbled and they pay for their sin, I will remember my covenant with Jacob and my covenant with Isaac and my covenant with Abraham and I will remember the land ... I will not reject them or abhor them so as to destroy them completely, breaking my covenant with them. I am the Lord their God. (Leviticus 26:40-44)

- *As they were given the Ten Commandments*: Later, when the Law was given to the people on Mount Horeb, the Lord reminded them that He was giving the land to them, as He had promised to Abraham, Isaac and Jacob (Deuteronomy 1:8). However, He knew that there was a danger that, in the midst of plenty, they would forget Him and the fact that He had delivered them from slavery. So Moses warned them of this:

When the Lord your God brings you into the land he swore to your fathers, to Abraham, Isaac and Jacob, to give you … be careful that you do not forget the Lord, who brought you out of Egypt, out of the land of slavery. (Deuteronomy 6:10, 12)

- *At the end of Moses' life:* As Moses neared the end of his life, and prepared to hand the reins over to Joshua, he warned the people of all the problems they would face when they entered the land. In particular, he warned them of the danger of idolatry, which subsequently did prove to be their undoing. One of his final acts was to renew the covenant between the Lord and the people. Again he invoked the original covenant with Abraham, Isaac and Jacob:

  "You are standing here in order to enter into a covenant with the Lord your God, a covenant the Lord is making with you this day and sealing with an oath, to confirm you this day as his people, that he may be your God as he promised you and as he swore to your fathers, Abraham, Isaac and Jacob." (Deuteronomy 29:12-13)

- *During the reign of David:* When David was confirmed as king over all Israel, he had the Ark of the Covenant brought back to Jerusalem. David composed a psalm of thanks to the Lord for His goodness. In that psalm he said of the Lord:

  "He remembers his covenant forever, the word he commanded, for a thousand generations, the covenant he made with Abraham, the oath he swore to Isaac. He confirmed it to Jacob as an everlasting covenant: 'To you I will give this land of Canaan as the portion you will inherit.'" (1 Chronicles 16:15-18)

- *During the reign of Ahab:* When Elijah stood against the prophets of Baal on Mount Carmel, he prayed to the Lord to send down fire on the sacrifice. In his prayer he addressed the Lord in terms of His relationship with the patriarchs: Abraham, Isaac and Jacob.

"O Lord, God of Abraham, Isaac and Israel, let it be known today that you are God in Israel and that I am your servant and have done all these things at your command." (1 Kings 18:36)

- *During the reign of Jehoahaz*: When the evil king Jehoahaz ruled over Israel, the nation was oppressed by Hazael, king of Aram. Nevertheless the Lord continued to be with them:

  The Lord was gracious to them and had compassion and showed concern for them because of his covenant with Abraham, Isaac and Jacob. To this day he has been unwilling to destroy them or banish them from his presence. (2 Kings 13:22-23)

The historical books, then, contain repeated references to the covenant made with the three great patriarchs and this was a golden thread that ran through Israel's chequered history.

However, for the covenant to be implemented they needed to walk in the ways of Abraham but first the northern kingdom of Israel, with its ten tribes, and then the southern kingdom of Judah, with the remaining two tribes, broke the covenant by following other gods. God had warned them repeatedly what would happen to them if they did this and both houses of Israel were judged and taken into exile. The prophets had foretold that this would happen.

The Abrahamic covenant in the prophetic books

Jeremiah prophesied to the southern two tribes that made up Judah, immediately prior to their exile in Babylon at the hands of Nebuchadnezzar. He warned them that this was going to happen because, like the northern ten tribes which made up Israel and who had earlier been taken into captivity by the Assyrians, they had abandoned the Lord and were worshipping other gods.

Both the house of Israel and the house of Judah have broken the covenant I made with their forefathers. Therefore, this is what the Lord says: 'I will bring on them a disaster they cannot escape.' (Jeremiah 11:10-11)

But yet, other prophets saw beyond the punishment of the nation to the time of her restoration and they viewed that restoration in terms of the Lord's promises to the patriarchs. For example, the Lord, through Isaiah declared that:

> "You, O Israel, my servant, Jacob, whom I have chosen, you descendants of Abraham my friend, I took you from the ends of the earth, from its farthest corners I called you. I said 'You are my servant;' I have chosen you and have not rejected you." (Isaiah 41:8-9)

Later in the prophecy, Isaiah spoke of the coming restoration of the nation, and he did this by reminding his hearers that they were the descendants of Abraham.

> "Listen to me, you who pursue righteousness and who seek the Lord: Look to the rock from which you were cut and to the quarry from which you were hewn: look to Abraham, your father and to Sarah, who gave you birth. When I called him he was but one, and I blessed him and made him many. The Lord will surely comfort Zion and will look with compassion on all her ruins; he will make her deserts like Eden, her wastelands like the garden of the Lord." (Isaiah 51:1-3)

Micah also foretold the reversal of the nation's misfortunes. And he saw that reversal in the context of the Lord's oath to Abraham:

> You will again have compassion on us; you will tread our sins underfoot and hurl all our iniquities into the depths of the sea. You will be true to Jacob, and show mercy to Abraham, as you pledged on oath to our fathers in days long ago. (Micah 7:19-20)

Even Jeremiah, whose message largely consisted of grim warnings of impending defeat, contains a glimmer of hope. That hope is the promise of a return from captivity at the end of 70 years.

> "I myself will gather the remnant of my flock out of all the countries where I have driven them and will bring them back to their pasture, where they will be fruitful and increase in number ... The days are coming," declares the Lord, "when I will raise up to David a righteous Branch, a King who will reign wisely and do what is just and right in the land. In his days Judah will be saved and Israel will live in safety." (Jeremiah 23:3-6)

Now that, of course, is a promise that will find fulfilment in the Lord Jesus Christ. So the ultimate blessing of the divided houses of Israel and Judah will take place when Jesus Christ, the Son of David, returns to set up His kingdom.

Further covenants with the nation

By the time the prophets were writing, the special relationship between the Lord and Israel had been strengthened by two further covenants in addition to the Abrahamic covenant – the covenant made through Moses on Mount Sinai and the covenant made with David concerning the kingship of Israel. What is the relationship between these covenants and the promises to Abraham? Paul gives us an explanation in Galatians:

> The law, introduced 430 years later, does not set aside the covenant previously established by God and thus do away with the promise. For if the inheritance depends on the law, then it no longer depends on a promise; but God in his grace gave it to Abraham through a promise. (Galatians 3:17-18)

This, of course, is part of a much longer argument that Paul developed to show that salvation is by grace through faith. However, it is important to note that the Law, given to Moses, and the covenant established at that time, did not replace the promise to Abraham. These additional covenants were added to put flesh on the bones of the original promise to the nation. The Law gave detailed instructions on how the descendants of Abraham were to live in line with the Lord's will. The kingship of David and his greater Son provided the mechanism for the civil system by which the Lord would rule over His redeemed people.[1]

The Lord, speaking through Jeremiah, emphasised the certainty of the fulfilment of His promises to the fathers:

> This is what the Lord says: "If I have not established my covenant with day and night and the fixed laws of heaven and earth, then I will reject the descendants of Jacob and David my servant and will not choose one of his sons to rule over the descendants of Abraham, Isaac and Jacob. For I will restore their fortunes and have compassion on them." (Jeremiah 33:25-26)

So both the historic books and the prophetic writings demonstrate the principles behind the Lord's covenant relationship with the nation – Abraham's seed. The unconditional promises originally made to Abraham, Isaac and Jacob would one day be fulfilled, but that time would be deferred for as long as the nation did not walk in the Lord's ways.

But did this mean that the deferral would be so indefinite as to make the promise nothing more than a pipe dream? Israel repeatedly failed the Lord. They insisted on worshipping the gods of the nations around them and refused to follow the Lord. But the prophets foresaw that the situation would change. Isaiah spoke of "those who pursue righteousness," Micah talked of their iniquities being hurled "into the depths of the sea." But how was this to be accomplished? What would bring about a change in Israel's behaviour?

Jeremiah saw that Judah was about to be exiled. He also saw that one day they would be brought back to the land; but he also saw beyond that, to

---

[1] For a detailed exploration of the covenants in Scripture, see *Covenants - Old and New* by William Henry.

the time when the Lord would make a new covenant with both houses of Israel.

The new covenant[2]

Jeremiah's announcement was really important.

> "The time is coming," declares the Lord, "when I will make a new covenant with the house of Israel and with the house of Judah. It will not be like the covenant I made with their forefathers when I took them by the hand to lead them out of Egypt because they broke my covenant, though I was a husband to them," declares the Lord ... "This is the covenant I will make with the house of Israel after that time," declares the Lord. "I will put my law in their minds and write it on their hearts. I will be their God and they will be my people." (Jeremiah 31:31-33)

So this new covenant, with both houses of Israel, will replace the old covenant, which had been repeatedly broken. And this new covenant, when God will write His laws on their hearts, would enable the original promise to Abraham to be fulfilled. They would be returned to the land in safety. The timing of this great event is linked with the coming of the great shepherd – the "righteous Branch" of Jeremiah 23:3-6 (quoted earlier on page 46).

This new covenant is one that will never be broken. Isaiah, Jeremiah and Ezekiel all declare it to be an "everlasting covenant."

> "In those days, at that time," declares the Lord, "the people of Israel and the people of Judah together will go in tears to seek the Lord their God. They will ask the way to Zion and turn their faces toward it. They will come and bind themselves to the Lord in an **everlasting covenant** that will not be forgotten." (Jeremiah 50:4-5)

---

[2] For more on the New Covenant see page 139.

This is what the Sovereign Lord says: "I will deal with you as you deserve, because you have despised my oath by breaking the covenant. Yet I will remember the covenant I made with you in the days of your youth, and I will establish an **everlasting covenant** with you." (Ezekiel 16:59-60)

Give ear and come to me; hear me, that your soul may live. I will make an **everlasting covenant** with you, my faithful love promised to David. (Isaiah 55:3)

So that is the guiding light through all Israel's dark times:

- God constantly reminding them of His everlasting promises to Abraham – the nation, the land, the blessings and that these promises will be fulfilled if they follow the Lord faithfully.
- God warning them that if they turn away to worship other gods and forsake Him, their generation would be punished and not inherit the promises.
- God reassuring them that, although they might be punished, the nation would not be wiped out because He will not abandon them.
- God informing them that, one day, as Jeremiah said, He will set up a new covenant with them and write His laws on their hearts.
- God declaring that the time of this new covenant with its supreme blessing would be when their Messiah, the Son of David, will come to set up His kingdom.

By the end of the Old Testament, Israel had returned to the land from the seventy year captivity but the area they occupied was not as extensive as God originally promised Abraham – the land from the river of Egypt to the Euphrates. However, they seem to have been cured of their tendency to idolatry and the temple worship was reinstated.

In chapter 9 of Nehemiah, which is really the last of the historical books chronologically, we find Israel confessing their sins and worshipping the

Lord. And the Levites launch into a hymn of praise to God. It includes the following statement:

> You are the Lord God, who chose Abram and brought him out of Ur of the Chaldeans and named him Abraham. You found his heart faithful to you and you made a covenant with him to give to his descendants the land of the Canaanites, Hittites, Amorites, Perizzites, Jebusites and Girgashites. You have kept your promise because you are righteous. (Nehemiah 9:7-8)

Israel were back in the land; they were worshiping the Lord; Jerusalem had been rebuilt. But everything in the garden was not rosy. Malachi, the final prophet in the OT, who wrote around the time of Nehemiah, berated Israel for the fact that, although they were offering their sacrifices, their hearts were not in it. He criticised Israel and their leaders for:

- bringing blind, crippled or diseased animals for sacrifices;
- giving false teaching to the people and operating a corrupt priesthood;
- not bringing in the full tithes as they were instructed;
- behaving unjustly in the national life.

They were very much going through the motions but in reality their hearts were far from God. So they did not have the full allocation of the land. There was no evidence of the new covenant in operation. Instead the Lord warned of judgment to come and pleaded with them to repent.

But after Malachi's prophecy God fell silent for 400 years. Eventually Israel, together with most of the civilised world, fell under the rule of Rome. The faithful ones in Israel were still waiting for their Messiah – the great king who would come to deliver them, set up His kingdom and implement that new covenant. The final words of Malachi are these:

> See, I will send you the prophet Elijah before that great and dreadful day of the Lord comes. He will turn the hearts of the fathers to their children and the hearts of the children to their

fathers; or else I will come and strike the land with a curse. (Malachi 4:5-6)

Then there were 400 years of silence.

And what is the event that breaks that silence? One day the old priest Zechariah, faithfully burning incense as he had always done in the temple, looked up and found himself face to face with Gabriel. The angel had a message that another old, childless couple were going to become parents. Zechariah and his wife, Elizabeth, like Abraham and Sarah before them, were going to have a son. A new phase was starting for Abraham's seed – something more amazing than anything the world had seen before. And who was this child? He was John the Baptist and Jesus told us that if the people had believed, he would have been Elijah (Matthew 17:12). This shows the link between the New Testament and Malachi's closing words.

So the story of Israel continues and the next chapter considers Abraham's seed in the Gospels.

Chapter 5
Abraham and his seed in the Gospels

Introduction

When we take an overview of the New Testament, we can split it into three time periods.

1. The Gospel Period
2. The Acts Period
3. The Post Acts Period

Associated with each of those periods are the documents which were written either in that period or about that period

- **The Gospel Period**
  Matthew, Mark, Luke, John
- **The Acts Period**
1) The Acts of the Apostles
2) *Letters to Jews*: Hebrews, James, 1 & 2 Peter, 1, 2 & 3 John, Jude, Revelation
3) *Paul's Earlier Letters*: Romans, 1 & 2 Corinthians, Galatians, 1 & 2 Thessalonians
- **The Post Acts Period**
  Paul's Later Letters: Ephesians, Philippians, Colossians, 1 & 2 Timothy, Titus, Philemon

The Gospels

By the time of the events described in the Gospels, the people of Israel, (i.e. the descendants of Abraham), had been back in the land for about 400 years. But once again they were under occupation by a foreign power – this time by the Romans. However, they were still fiercely nationalistic, and they were also very religious. They were very proud of their heritage, and their physical descent from Abraham was very important to them. They were all keen to trace their ancestry back to Abraham. So physically, to be the "seed of Abraham," and to be circumcised as a sign of the covenant as laid down by God to Abraham 1500 years earlier, were still of utmost importance to the Jews. They were still the favoured nation, they had the promises from God, they had the covenants, they felt superior to the Gentile nations around them, and they certainly felt superior to the Roman forces that occupied them.

Who is referred to as the "seed of Abraham"?

When we turn to the very beginning of the New Testament, the first verse of Matthew's Gospel says:

> A record of the genealogy of Jesus Christ the son of David, the son of Abraham.

The very first fact that is established in the Gospels is the physical genealogy of Jesus going back (through King David) to Abraham. It was most important to the Jews that this was established at the outset. Jesus was truly the "seed of Abraham" in a physical sense. Paul refers to this in Galatians 3:16 (one of his earlier letters) which says:

> The promises were spoken to Abraham and to his seed. The Scripture does not say "and to seeds", meaning many people, but "and to your seed", meaning one person, who is Christ.

Abraham and his seed   54

Although this is a difficult verse to understand entirely (see the Appendix), what is clear is that Jesus is referred to as "the seed of Abraham", and that this was meant literally. Also, we know historically that the Jews collectively were considered to be "the seed of Abraham". So both Christ individually, and the nation of Israel collectively, are known as "the seed of Abraham".

However, although it is very clear that the Jews themselves considered that proving their ancestry back to Abraham was of utmost importance, was this also true of the Lord Jesus Himself? Did He consider this literal and physical heritage was as important as they did? The Jews thought this was a real blessing, and something to be prized above all else. Did He agree? We will answer these questions as we look at the Gospels.

Mary's song and Zechariah's song

At the beginning of Luke's Gospel, the importance of being a descendant of Abraham is made very clear. First we have Mary's song, in which she praised the Lord, but she finished by saying:

> "He has helped his servant Israel, remembering to be merciful to Abraham and his descendants for ever, even as he said to our fathers." (Luke 1:54-55)

When Mary knew she was to become the mother of the Son of God, her first reaction was to praise God, to rejoice, and to refer to Abraham and the promises made to him and his descendants for ever.
A few verses later we have Zechariah's song - which is the first thing he said after his son was born and his speech was restored. He was filled with the Holy Spirit, and said:

> "Praise be to the Lord, the God of Israel, because he has come and has redeemed his people. He has raised up a horn of salvation for us ... to show mercy to our fathers and to remember his holy covenant, the oath he swore to our father Abraham: to rescue us from the hand of our enemies, and to enable us to serve him

without fear in holiness and righteousness before him all our days." (Luke 1:68-69,72-75)

Similar to Mary, his first reaction (to the birth of John) was to praise God, to rejoice, and to refer to the holy covenant given to Abraham - the oath that God had sworn to him.

Whenever the Jews were thankful to God, they tended to think immediately of Abraham, and the promises that God had made to him and his descendants forever. The promises were to the seed of Abraham - and of course, *they* were the seed of Abraham! As Paul was later to say about them:

> Theirs is the adoption as sons; theirs the divine glory, the covenants, the receiving of the law, the temple worship and the promises. Theirs are the patriarchs, and from them is traced the human ancestry of Christ, who is God over all, for ever praised! Amen. (Romans 9:4-5)

Here Paul summarised the way the Jews felt about their position with God, the fact that they were His favoured nation, and that they were descended from the patriarchs (Abraham, Isaac and Jacob) as was Christ Himself. And this nationalistic pride was just the same in the Gospel Period.

John the Baptist

John the Baptist gives us some insight into the way the Jews thought of themselves, and particularly the Pharisees and Sadducees, the leaders who everyone else looked up to during the Gospel Period. Matthew 3:7-10 refers to John when he was baptising people in the river Jordan, and says:

> But when he saw many of the Pharisees and Sadducees coming to where he was baptising, he said to them: "You brood of vipers. Who warned you to flee from the coming wrath? Produce fruit

Abraham and his seed   56

in keeping with repentance. And do not think you can say to yourselves, 'We have Abraham as our father.' I tell you that out of these stones God can raise up children for Abraham. The axe is already at the root of the trees, and every tree that does not produce good fruit will be cut down and thrown into the fire."

This also comes in Luke 3:7-9, which records that John spoke to the crowds, (not just the Pharisees and Sadducees), and called them all a brood of vipers! John certainly was not very complimentary to many of the Jews who came to see him baptising, and to listen to what he had to say. He was very blunt in what he said.

In these verses he refuted the popular idea that racial descent from Abraham, in and of itself, brought divine blessing. Instead, he told them that having Abraham as their father was of no value, unless they also "produced fruit in keeping with repentance." Basically, their pedigree was worthless unless it was combined with a change of heart, producing good fruit, and obedience to God and His requirements. Only then would they be blessed by God. In other words, not only did they have to be physically descended from Abraham, they also had to put their faith into practice, just as Abraham did.

This was the first challenge to their traditionally held view, and it must have come like a bombshell to the Jews, especially the leaders, who were so used to relying wholly on their physical ancestry for their standing with God, rather than thinking about pleasing God in the way they behaved.

As mentioned in the introduction, these Jews were also very concerned with physical circumcision. This was as important to them as their physical descent from Abraham. And yet, again, they should have known better. In several places in the Old Testament it was made clear that God was concerned with the circumcision of their hearts rather than their bodies (Deuteronomy 10:16; 30:6; Jeremiah 4:4). What was important to God was not the outward show, but rather their inner selves. He wanted them to be genuine. He wanted them to love Him with all their hearts, all their minds and all their strength. In fact, when Jesus was asked what the greatest commandment was, this was the first part of His answer (Mark 12:29-31). This should have been the inner meaning of the outward show of circumcision.

This is exactly what Paul wrote in his letter to the Romans. He said:

> A man is not a Jew if he is only one outwardly, nor is circumcision merely outward and physical. No, a man is a Jew if he is one inwardly; and circumcision is circumcision of the heart. (Romans 2:28-29)

Jesus Christ

Following on from John the Baptist and his message to the Jews, what was Jesus' attitude towards this view the Jews had of themselves? Did He also consider being a Jew (the seed of Abraham) was of such importance?

And what was His attitude towards the Gentiles? Until now, we have made no mention of Gentiles – what their position was, and how they were viewed in the Gospel Period – apart from the fact that the Jews felt superior to the surrounding Gentile nations, and superior to the Romans, even though they were the occupying force in Israel at that time.

Jesus' attitude to being a Jew

First we will consider whether being a Jew was important to the Lord. In Luke 13:16, after Jesus had healed a crippled woman, He said to His critics:

> "Then should not this woman, *a daughter of Abraham*, whom Satan has kept bound for eighteen long years, be set free on the Sabbath day from what bound her?"

The fact that she was a daughter of Abraham was emphasised by the Lord, which implies it was as important to Him as it was to His critics in the synagogue. Also, a little later, in Luke 19:9, after Zacchaeus the tax collector had made a profession of faith, Jesus said to him:

> "Today salvation has come to this house, because this man, too, is a *son of Abraham*."

Again, the fact that Zacchaeus was a son of Abraham was important to the Lord. Tax collectors were generally despised by the Jews as being in the pay of the hated Romans, and therefore, in their eyes they were "sinners", and not worth spending any time with. When Jesus said He wanted to go to his house as a guest, the Jews standing around therefore muttered against Him. However, when Zacchaeus had a dramatic change of heart, Jesus pointed out to these critical Jews that Zacchaeus was also a son of Abraham. It was important. Not only that, but he was counted a *true* son of Abraham, on account of his faith.

Jesus' Attitude to Gentiles

Next, what was the Lord's view of the Gentiles? In Matthew 10:5-6 we can see the Lord's attitude towards preaching to the Gentiles:

> These twelve Jesus sent out with the following instructions: "Do not go among the Gentiles or enter any town of the Samaritans. Go rather to the lost sheep of Israel. As you go, preach this message: 'The kingdom of heaven is near.'"

Here it is quite clear that Jesus did not want His disciples to go preaching to the Gentiles.

As we saw from the Old Testament, the promise given to Abraham was that he would be made into a great nation, and that through his seed all nations on earth would be blessed. But during the Gospel Period they were to concentrate on preaching to "the lost sheep of Israel". They were to concentrate on getting Israel back on track first, before they were to be sent out to the Gentiles.

In John 12:20-22 we have a small incident recorded that is very easy to read over, but, again, it shows the Lord's attitude towards the Gentiles. It says:

> Now there were some Greeks among those who went up to worship at the Feast. They came to Philip, who was from Bethsaida in Galilee, with a request. "Sir", they said, "we would like to see Jesus." Philip went to tell Andrew; Andrew and Philip in turn told Jesus.

What was Jesus' response to these Gentiles? We do not know, as the Scriptures say nothing more about these Greeks. However, on the face of it He seemingly ignored this request, and instead began to talk about His impending sacrifice on the cross.

However, Jesus does interact with two Gentiles in the Gospels, but these are the *only* two. And there are good reasons for Him dealing with both of these.

The first was a Roman centurion, recorded in Luke 7. He sent some Jewish elders to ask Jesus to heal his servant who was about to die. They pleaded with the Lord to do this, as the centurion loved their nation and had built them their local synagogue. Those Gentiles who treated the Jews well were, in return, to be blessed by the Jews, as stated in the Abrahamic covenant (Genesis 12:3). So, because of this, Jesus went to heal his servant. Before He arrived, however, the centurion said He need not trouble Himself to go there, as he knew Jesus could just say the word, and his servant would be healed. Jesus was amazed and said "I have not found such great faith even in Israel." He was amazed because, in theory, it should have been the Jews who had the greater faith, as they were the ones who had all the advantages, as we have seen. However, here was a Gentile who had blessed the Jews by building them a synagogue, and so he received a blessing from Jesus in return.

The other Gentile the Lord had dealings with was a Canaanite woman. She cried after Jesus, saying:

> "Lord, Son of David, have mercy on me! My daughter is suffering terribly from demon-possession". (Matthew 15:22)

At first Jesus ignored her, just like the Greeks we looked at earlier. The disciples urged Him to send her away as she kept making a nuisance of herself, and crying out after them. She was obviously very persistent! The Lord's response was to say to the disciples, (but of course, in the woman's hearing):

> "I was sent only to the lost sheep of Israel." (Matthew 15:24)

As a result, she came and kneeled at the Lord's feet and pleaded with Him to help her. He told her that it was not right to toss the children's bread to their dogs. She immediately understood what He meant, and agreed with Him, but countered by saying "but even the dogs eat the crumbs that fall from their master's table." So Jesus answered her and said:

> "Woman, you have great faith! Your request is granted." And her daughter was healed from that very hour. (Matthew 15:28)

Although she was a Gentile, she knew her position. She knew that Gentiles were to be blessed through the Jews, as had been promised to Abraham, and she appealed to the Lord on those grounds. She, like the centurion[3], had great faith, and she obviously knew the Old Testament scriptures, and knew her own position. In response, Jesus blessed her and healed her daughter.

---

[3] This woman and the centurion are examples of what the New Testament calls God-fearing Gentiles. These attended the synagogues, sitting in a separate section from the Jews. Cornelius was one such Gentile, Acts 10:1-2.

However, these two incidents are exceptions. Each had specific reasons why the Lord dealt with them. They were unusual. Other than these, we have no record of Him having any other dealings with Gentiles (other than Pilate of course) while He was on earth. As He said Himself, He was sent only to the lost sheep of Israel – the seed of Abraham.

The seed of Abraham in John 8

Returning to the subject of the Jews' own view of the importance of their heritage, there is an interesting passage in John 8:31-41, part of which talks about their pride in being descendants of Abraham.

In this passage it is made very clear, once again, how confident these Jews were in their natural descent from Abraham. It meant everything to them. They also claimed that they had never been slaves of anyone, conveniently forgetting the four hundred years as slaves in Egypt, and the Assyrian captivity of the northern kingdom, and the Babylonian captivity of the southern kingdom. And they also seemed to have forgotten, temporarily, that they were at that very time, under Roman occupation. Technically they were not slaves, but neither were they free to do as they chose.

However, Jesus ignored all this in His response, and cut to the heart of the matter, which was sin. He explained that everyone who sins is a slave to sin. They would only be free when they were freed from sin.

Then He took up the subject of them being Abraham's children (his seed). He told them that if they were truly Abraham's seed they would do the things Abraham had done. Not only was physical descent important – they had to have faith, and put it into practice, just like Abraham. Jesus then went on to make it quite clear that He meant the devil when He referred to their father.

Jesus reinforced what John the Baptist had said, earlier, while he was baptising by the river Jordan. He had told them that unless they "produced fruit in keeping with repentance" they could not rely on calling

Abraham their father. In other words, He too hinted that everyone who was physically descended from Abraham was not necessarily Abraham's true seed. They had to repent and produce fruit.

So in this passage in John 8:31-41, Jesus made it clear that if they had been Abraham's true children they would have believed in Him. As it was, He told them that their true father was the devil.

Did any of the Jews believe that He was the Christ, the Son of God? The answer is that some did, but most did not. However, the Jewish leadership, in the main, did not listen and so, ultimately, His message was rejected, and they decided to put Him to death.

The new covenant[4]

The night before He died, Jesus talked about the "new covenant" for the very first time. He mentioned this to His disciples in the upper room where they celebrated the Passover together. Luke 22:20 says:

> In the same way, after the supper he took the cup, saying, "This cup is the new covenant in my blood, which is poured out for you."

And there are similar passages in Matthew and Mark's Gospels. Here, Jesus reminded them of the prophecy in Jeremiah 31:31-34.

This new covenant was to be with the "house of Israel" and the "house of Judah"; i.e. the seed of Abraham. However, when Jesus referred to this at the last supper, He made no mention of when this would happen. He never said when the old covenant would pass away, and when the new covenant would come in. This was left for those coming afterwards to explain. However, in the Gospel Period, there was just a hint that things were going to change and that the implementation of the new covenant was potentially imminent.

---

[4] For more on the New Covenant see page 139.

Who were the true seed of Abraham in the Gospels?

So to conclude, who were the true seed of Abraham in the Gospels? First and foremost, Jesus Christ was the true seed. But also the physical descendants of Abraham, through Isaac and Jacob *could* be the true seed, as long as they repented of their sin, and had an active faith like Abraham so that they produced fruit in keeping with repentance.

But, where did the Gentiles fit into this? Were they ever described as the seed of Abraham in the Gospels? As we have seen, there is very little said at all about Gentiles during the Gospel Period. The Lord actually avoided contact with the Gentiles, and we only have a record of Him interacting with two specific Gentiles, who were exceptions to the rule. Both are described as having great faith, but this did not make either of them into a "spiritual seed of Abraham". Nowhere is this suggested in the Gospels, and there is no hint that the Lord said any such thing either to the centurion, or to the Canaanite woman. To be the seed of Abraham they had to be physically descended from him, and have an active faith like him.

But at the end of the Gospels we have the rejection of the Lord Jesus by the people of Israel and their leaders. He was handed over to the Romans and crucified. But on the third day He rose again and appeared to His disciples over a period of 40 days, teaching and instructing them. So what was the message they were to take to the people of Israel? Was there any future for the seed of Abraham after they had failed to recognise the One God had sent to them? The continued unfolding of God's purposes is contained in the Acts of the Apostles, which is the subject of the next chapter.

Chapter 6

Abraham and his seed in the Acts of the Apostles

Introduction

We have seen how dominant Abraham's seed was in the Gospel Period and in this chapter we shall consider the position they occupied in Luke's second treatise – the Acts of the Apostles. In chapter seven we shall consider their role in the letters written during the Acts Period, and in chapter eight we will look at their role in the Post Acts Period.

Many have argued that the people of Israel (the seed of Abraham) were moved off the scene at the end of the Gospels. Their sin of rejecting and crucifying their Messiah ensured that they no longer held a major place in the plans and purposes of God, but is that correct? Daniel wrote of the years that were decreed for his people (the Jews) and his holy city (Jerusalem). Had those years run their course by the crucifixion or were his people and his city still the major players in God's dealings with mankind?

If we compare the frequencies of certain words used in the Gospels and the Acts of the Apostles we can construct the following table.

	The Gospels	The Acts of the Apostles
	89 chapters	28 chapters
Abraham	34	8
Israel / Israelite	31	21
Jew / Jews / Jewish	72	81
Jerusalem	66	61

It is clear that, although there are less direct references to Abraham, his seed, the people of Israel, are still very prominent.

Abraham in Acts

As Peter and the other apostles preached the message of the Lord Jesus in Acts, they stressed the historic link with Abraham, Isaac and Jacob. For example, in his speech to the Jews in the temple, following the healing of the crippled beggar, Peter referred to God as "The God of Abraham, Isaac and Jacob" (Acts 3:13). And later he told the Jews that:

> "… you are heirs of the prophets and of the covenant God made with your fathers. He said to Abraham, 'Through your offspring all peoples on earth will be blessed.'" (Acts 3:25)

In Acts 7, Stephen commenced his defence before the high priest and the Sanhedrin by providing a detailed history of the nation starting with the time when the God of glory appeared to Abraham "in Mesopotamia, before he lived in Haran" (Acts 7:2), describing the promise of a land and a child (Acts 7:5), the giving of the covenant of circumcision and the births of Isaac and Jacob (Acts 7:8).

He then described God appearing to Moses, and introducing Himself in terms of His relationship with the patriarchs:

"I am the God of your fathers, the God of Abraham, Isaac and Jacob." (Acts 7:32)

Peter and Stephen, then, were careful to present the good news in its historical context. The God whom they were proclaiming was still the God of Abraham, Isaac and Jacob and the message of the risen Jesus was for the seed of Abraham.

The Seed of Abraham in Acts

Although there are only eight direct references to Abraham in Acts, we can see from the table on page 67 that there are many more references to the seed of Abraham; i.e. the people of Israel, the Jews. That table alone shows that these people, the seed of Abraham, still had a significant place in the Acts of the Apostles. As we shall see, the Jews and Jerusalem still occupied centre stage during the Acts Period.

The Acts of the Apostles opens with three significant events:

- a question,
- a replacement, and
- a feast.

The question

After being taught by the risen Saviour for 40 days, and having had their minds opened by Christ so that they could understand the Scriptures (Luke 24:45), the apostles asked Him:

"Lord, are you at this time going to restore the kingdom to *Israel*?" (Acts 1:6)

He did not dismiss the question, but said it was not for them to know the date or time. However, He did tell them to be His witnesses, first in

Jerusalem and then in Judea. Thus the people in the city and in the land of Israel were still first.

The replacement

We then read of the need to replace Judas; that another was to take his place of leadership (Acts 1:21-26). Why was this? During His time on earth, the Lord had told them:

> "I tell you the truth, at the renewal of all things, when the Son of Man sits on his glorious throne, you who have followed me will also sit on twelve thrones, judging the twelve tribes of *Israel*." (Matthew 19:28)

So Israel was still prominent, and Judas' vacant seat needed to be filled, as there could not be eleven judging the twelve tribes of Israel.

The feast

Acts chapter 2 starts off with the *Jewish* feast of Pentecost. We must remember that Pentecost was a 'Jewish' feast, as were the others listed in Leviticus 23. However, as if to draw our attention to this, we read in Acts 2:5 that "There were staying in Jerusalem *God-fearing Jews* from every nation under heaven." And when Peter spoke to these people he addressed them as:

- Fellow Jews (Acts 2:14);
- Men of Israel (Acts 2:22);
- Brothers (a term he would, at that time, not have used of Gentiles; Acts 2:29).

At the end of Peter's speech we read that about 3,000 were saved (Acts 2:41), and these were all Jews; there was not one Gentile among them.

They carried on preaching and teaching "in the temple courts" and we read that the Lord added to their number daily (Acts 2:46-47), but the people added were all Jews.

And by Acts 4:4 we read that "the number of men grew to about 5,000" but, again ... these were all Jewish men: there were no Gentiles amongst them.

From this alone we can see that the seed of Abraham had not been put aside by God at the start of Acts.

Peter's message to Abraham's seed

What was the message that Peter was trying to put across to his Jewish hearers?[5] His worldview was that the Lord Jesus had come to Israel as their Messiah ("Christ"), in fulfilment of Old Testament prophecy to Israel. They, however, had rejected Him, and crucified Him. But God had raised Him from the dead and, if they repented of their rejection of Him, He would return, restore the kingdom to Israel and enable the nation to fulfil their mission as a kingdom of priests, bringing God's blessing to the rest of the world. This was the means by which the Lord would fulfil His covenant promises to Abraham.

For example, Peter concluded his first sermon at Pentecost with this clear declaration:

> Therefore, let all Israel be assured of this: God has made this Jesus, whom you crucified, both Lord and Christ. (Acts 2:36)

Peter linked the promised return of the Lord Jesus with the Abrahamic covenant in his second speech in Acts 3. He instructed the people to:

---

[5] For a discussion of the message of the apostles during the book of the Acts of the Apostles, see *The Speeches in Acts* by William Henry.

Repent, then… that times of refreshing may come from the Lord, and that he may send the Christ, who has been appointed for you – even Jesus. He must remain in heaven until the time comes for God to restore everything, as he promised long ago through his holy prophets…And you are the heirs of the prophets and of the covenant God made with your fathers. He said to Abraham, "Through your offspring all peoples on earth will be blessed," (Acts 3:19-21, 25)

The Messiahship of Jesus was the nub of the message of Peter and the other disciples at that time. At the end of Acts 5, after the disciples had been flogged by the Jews for continuing to preach in the name of Jesus, Luke sums up the position by saying:

Day after day in the temple courts and from house to house, they never stopped teaching and proclaiming the good news that Jesus is the Christ. (Acts 5:42)

Peter believed that the other nations of the earth would be blessed through Abraham's seed *after* the kingdom was established. However, the Lord wanted to show Peter that, in fact, He wanted to bring Gentiles into blessing at that time.

The first Gentile

The first example of a Gentile being blessed in Acts is in chapter 10, where we encounter Cornelius, a God-fearing Gentile. The Lord made it very clear that He wanted Peter to go to Caesarea to meet Cornelius. He gave Peter a vision of a sheet descending from heaven, which contained all manner of animals. Peter was instructed to "kill and eat" but he refused to do so because they were unclean according to the Law of Moses. Peter was then informed by the Lord:

"Do not call anything impure that God has made clean." (Acts 10:15)

This vision was repeated three times after which Peter was told explicitly that three men were looking for him and that he was to go with them (Acts 10:20).

Peter went with the men and when he arrived at Cornelius' home we learn that the meaning of the vision was to show Peter that he "should not call any man impure or unclean" (Acts 10:28). Peter told the gathered company of Gentiles about Christ and when they believed, the Holy Spirit came upon them (Acts 10:43-44).

The Jewish believers who had come with Peter were astonished when this happened and when news of this visit to a Gentile, an uncircumcised man, reached Jerusalem, Peter was criticised.

> So when Peter went up to Jerusalem, the circumcised believers criticised him and said, "You went into the house of uncircumcised men and ate with them." (Acts 11:2-3)

Peter explained everything: the vision he had had, the Holy Spirit's instructions, his conversation with Cornelius, the Gentiles coming to faith in Christ and the Holy Spirit coming upon them. When the circumcised believers (who probably included James and many of the Apostles) heard this they had no further objections and praised God (Acts 11:18).

We have no record in the Scriptures of Peter going to another Gentile or even of having much contact with them. He did visit the church at Antioch in Syria, but in doing so he caused problems (Galatians 2:11-16), and some think he may have gone to Babylon (1 Peter 5:13). He could possibly have done so because we know from history that there was a large Jewish community there and he may have visited them.

Also we read nothing of Peter or the other Apostles, or any of the Jewish Christians in Jerusalem, going to any further Gentiles. However, something rather unexpected happened. Earlier, after the stoning of Stephen, "great persecution broke out against the church at Jerusalem, and all except the Apostles were scattered" (Acts 8:1).

Now those who had been scattered by the persecution in connection with Stephen travelled as far as Phoenicia, Cyprus and Antioch, telling the message only to Jews. Some of them, however, men from Cyprus and Cyrene, went to Antioch and began to speak to Greeks also, telling them the good news about the Lord Jesus. The Lord's hand was with them, and a great number of people believed and turned to the Lord. (Acts 11:19-21)

Eventually news of this reached the Jerusalem church and it seems they were, again, concerned about non-Jews coming into the Christian fold and so they sent Barnabas to Antioch (Acts 11:22). They saw the good work being done there among the Gentiles with a great number of people believing and turning to the Lord. Then Barnabas went to Tarsus to look for Saul, later to be called Paul (Acts 11:24-25). But why did Barnabas go to find Paul?

We read of Paul's conversion in Acts 9. The arch-persecutor of the church became arguably its greatest apostle. Immediately after his encounter with the Lord Jesus on the Damascus road, Paul began to preach powerfully in the synagogues in Damascus, "that Jesus is the Son of God" (Acts 9:20). So effective was his preaching that the Jews conspired to kill him. However, he was able to escape and return to his home city of Tarsus (Acts 9:30). It is important, though, that we pay special attention to the commission Christ gave him. The Lord told Ananias about Paul. He said:

"This man is my chosen instrument to carry my name before the Gentiles and their kings and before the people of Israel." (Acts 9:15)

Note again, "the people of Israel", as well as the Gentiles. At this point Paul had a dual ministry: to the Gentiles and to the Jews. So, we may ask, what was the relationship between those 'Gentiles' of the Acts Period and the 'Jews' of that time? We will deal with that issue in the next chapter.

Paul's message to Abraham's seed

So what was Paul's message to the Jews? Was it the same as that of Peter? When we read of the events after Paul's conversion we find that the same critically important truth lay at the heart of Paul's teaching – that Jesus is the Christ. Immediately after his conversion we find Paul among the Christians in Damascus.

> At once he began to preach in the synagogues that Jesus is the Son of God … Saul grew more and more powerful and baffled the Jews living in Damascus by proving that Jesus is the Christ. (Acts 9:20, 22)

Paul, the Pharisee, with his vast knowledge of the Hebrew Bible (the Old Testament) and his newly opened eyes, was able to prove that Jesus was the One who had been foretold by the prophets. The people of Israel and the God-fearing Gentiles who had aligned themselves with the God of Israel, were the ones to whom this good news was directed.

> "Brothers, children of Abraham, and you God-fearing Gentiles, it is to us that this message of salvation has been sent. The people of Jerusalem and their rulers did not recognise Jesus, yet in condemning him they fulfilled the words of the prophets that are read every Sabbath… We tell you the good news: What God had promised our fathers he has fulfilled in us their children, by raising up Jesus." (Acts 13:26-27, 32-33)

The message of Paul, then, echoed the message of Peter: the first priority was the Jewish people, to show them that Jesus was their Messiah and that the fulfilment of the promises made to the fathers was dependent on their acceptance of that fact.

The remainder of the Acts of the Apostles focuses on the travels and ministry of Paul.

Off to Jerusalem

Having spent a year in Antioch, Paul and Barnabas took a gift for the poor to Jerusalem (Acts 11:25-30). There they met with James, Peter and John and came to an agreement. This was that Paul and Barnabas would go to the Gentiles and Peter, James and John would go to the Jews (Galatians 2:9). However, we need to be aware that the word translated 'Gentiles' is the word *ethnos*, which could refer to Gentile nations, or lands. From what is recorded in the Acts of the Apostles, and elsewhere, it seems they agreed that Paul and Barnabas should go to the Gentile nations and carry out Paul's commission to "the Gentiles ... and the people of Israel"; i.e. the dispersed of Israel, those scattered throughout the Roman Empire and beyond. Peter, James and John, on the other hand, were mainly to reside in Jerusalem and Judea, and witness to the Jews who lived there or those Jews of the dispersion who visited Jerusalem for feast days. Later, Peter, James and John were to write letters to those scattered Jews (e.g. see James 1:1; 1 Peter 1:1).

Paul's first missionary journey

Although Paul was commissioned to go to "the Gentiles ... and the people of Israel", it is evident from what is written in the Acts of the Apostles that the Jews had first place. For example, we read:

> When they arrived at Salamis, they proclaimed the word of God in the *Jewish synagogues*. (Acts 13:5)

> From Perga they went on to Pisidian Antioch. On the Sabbath they entered the *synagogue* and sat down. (Acts 13:14)

> At Iconium Paul and Barnabas went *as usual* into *the Jewish synagogue*. (Acts 14:1)

From this last reference we see that going to the Jewish synagogue was Paul's habitual practice, and this continued throughout Acts:-

As his custom was, Paul went into *the synagogue*, and on three Sabbath days, he reasoned with them from the Scriptures. (Acts 17:2)

Every Sabbath he reasoned in *the synagogue*, trying to persuade Jews and Greeks. (Acts 18:4)

Paul entered *the synagogue* and spoke boldly there *for three months*, arguing persuasively about the kingdom of God. (Acts 19:8)

Jerusalem and Jews

That the seed of Abraham were still dominant is very clear from events described in Acts 15. After their first missionary journey Paul and Barnabas returned to Antioch. While there, some Jews from Judea arrived in Antioch and started to teach that unless the Gentiles were circumcised, they could not be saved (Acts 15:1). The church at Antioch sent Paul and Barnabas to "the apostles and elders" in Jerusalem, for them to make a decision on the issue.

On arriving in Jerusalem, they were faced with the same problem when some believers who belonged to the Pharisees said that

"The Gentiles must be circumcised and required to obey the law of Moses." (Acts 15:5)

The "apostles and elders" in Jerusalem met to discuss this issue and decided that the Gentiles needed neither to be circumcised nor to keep the Law of Moses. However, we should note that the "apostles and elders" were all Jews (the seed of Abraham), and included people like James, the Lord's brother (Acts 15:6,13). These were the people who made the decisions and the centre for decision making was Jerusalem.

In fact, if we read through the Acts of the Apostles, and the letters written during that time, we will see that 'all' the Christian leaders, teachers and evangelists, were of the seed of Abraham; i.e. Jews. We may wonder why this was so. One possibility may be found in Romans 3:1-2 where we read:

> What advantage, then, is there in being a Jew, or what value is there in circumcision? *Much in every way!* First of all, they have been entrusted with the very words of God.

Thus it was the Jewish Christians who knew the Scriptures. The new Gentile converts did not, and had much to learn about the character of God and what the Scriptures taught. Therefore the Jewish Christians were better equipped for leading, evangelising and teaching.

Tens of thousands of Jews

As we follow Paul through his journeys we see him, as usual in new places, going first to the Jews at their synagogues or at their meeting places (e.g. in Philippi – Acts 16:13; in Thessalonica – Acts 17:1-3; in Berea – Acts 17:10; Athens – Acts 17:17; Corinth – 18:4). If there was opposition, as there frequently was, or if there were other reasons, he would then preach to the Gentiles.

After his third missionary journey he again went up to Jerusalem to report to James and the elders, telling them what God had done among the Gentile nations (Acts 21:19). They were pleased and praised God, and then told Paul:

> "You see, brother, how many *thousands of Jews* have believed, and all of them are zealous for the law." (Acts 21:20)

However, the Greek word translated 'thousands' is *murias* (which gives us 'myriads') which means 'tens of thousands' and is translated so in Jude 14 and Revelation 5:11 (*KJV*). In fact, in Acts 19:19, we have 'five myriads' which is translated 'fifty thousand'.

It is therefore clear that the seed of Abraham was still dominant at this late stage in the Acts Period. All the apostles and elders were from the people of Israel and tens of thousands of Jews believed in Christ.

Paul imprisoned

Shortly after his conversation with James, Paul was arrested and escorted to Caesarea. He first appeared before Felix and then, when the new governor arrived, he was called to give an account of himself to Festus, and King Agrippa was also present. In his defence we read that Paul stated:

> "And now it is because of my hope in what God has promised *our fathers* that I am on trial today. This is the *promise* our *twelve tribes* are hoping to see fulfilled as they earnestly serve God day and night." (Acts 26:6-7)

It is important to note that Paul refers to:

- 'our fathers' (namely Abraham, Isaac and Jacob)
- the 'twelve tribes', and
- the 'promise' made to the fathers, that the twelve tribes would be a nation, have a land, be blessed and be a blessing to other (Gentile) nations.

Even in the closing chapters of Acts, Paul's focus remained on the hope of Israel. The message of Peter and Paul to Jews and the God-fearers who linked themselves with Israel and the Jewish faith was that Jesus of Nazareth, whom they had crucified, was their Messiah, whose coming had been predicted in the Old Testament and who would return to set up His kingdom, restore Israel and implement the promises made to Abraham, Isaac and Jacob. This was the hope of Israel and the primary emphasis of Paul's message.

Paul in Rome

Paul had never visited Rome (at least not since his conversion). When he wrote to the Roman church from Corinth on his third missionary journey (Acts 20:2) he expressed his desire to visit them:

> But now that there is no more place for me to work in these regions, and since I have been longing for many years to see you, I plan to do so when I go to Spain. I hope to visit you while passing through and to have you assist me on my journey there, after I have enjoyed your company for a while. (Romans 15:23-24)

However, when he did finally arrive at Rome in Acts 28, it was as a prisoner of the Romans. We are told that the first people Paul called together were the "leaders of the *Jews*" (Acts 28:17), and he told them:

> "For this reason I have asked to see you and talk with you. It is because of *the hope of Israel* that I am bound with this chain." (Acts 28:20)

Here, in the last chapter of Acts, Paul spoke again about 'the hope of *Israel*'. And as we read further we see Paul tried to convince them (i.e. the leaders of the Jews) about Jesus, basing his arguments on "the Law of Moses and the Prophets" (Acts 28:23).

A change

So far in this chapter we have been at pains to point out the positives pertaining to the seed of Abraham. They were still God's people throughout the time covered by the Acts of the Apostles. However, there was an undercurrent of opposition, mainly from the Jewish leadership. We see this in Acts 4 and 5 when Peter and John were arrested and brought before the Sanhedrin: they were imprisoned and flogged (Acts 5:40). Stephen was stoned and great persecution broke out against the church in Jerusalem (Acts 8:1). James was killed by Herod and Peter imprisoned (Acts 12:1-4). Paul was abused by the Jews at Pisidian Antioch (Acts 13:45); he was stoned by Jews from Antioch and Iconium (Acts 14:19); and so on. On his last visit to Jerusalem he had to be rescued from the Jews by the Roman commander and escorted out of Jerusalem to safety in Caesarea (Acts 21:30-32; 23:23-24).

When we read about Christians suffering in the New Testament letters, there is a tendency for us to think the Christians were Gentiles and that the perpetrators were the Romans, but that was not the case. When we read about the suffering and persecution it is mainly Jewish Christians suffering at the hands of other Jews, especially the Jewish leadership. What was it the Lord Jesus said?

> "But before all this, they will lay hands on you and persecute you. They will deliver you to synagogues and prisons, and you will be brought before kings and governors, and all on account of my name ... You will be betrayed even by parents, brothers, relatives and friends, and they will put some of you to death." (Luke 21:12,16)

Here the Lord told the (Jewish) disciples they would be persecuted even by Jews. In many ways this persecution came to a head at the end of the Acts of the Apostles. The Jews in Rome did no better than those elsewhere; some believed what Paul taught about Jesus, and some did not. Paul was thus inspired to utter Isaiah's judgemental prophecy ... for the last time. The Lord had quoted it at the Jews two or three times when He was on earth, and Paul had referred to it earlier. However, here, at the end of Acts, is that last time we read it.

> "Go to this people and say,
> 'You will be ever hearing but never understanding;
>   you will be ever seeing but never perceiving.'
> For this people's heart has become calloused;
>   they hardly hear with their ears,
>   and they have closed their eyes.

Otherwise they might see with their eyes,
    hear with their ears,
    understand with their hearts
and turn, and I would heal them."
(Acts 28:26-27; quoting Isaiah 6:9-10[6])

What was the significance of the final pronouncement of this prophecy, and the words which followed, "That God's salvation has been sent to the Gentiles, and they will listen" (Acts 28:28)? Before we can answer that question, we will need to look at the place of the seed of Abraham in the letters written during the time covered by the Acts of the Apostles.

---

[6] For more on Isaiah 6 and its use in Acts 28, see page 134.

Chapter 7

Abraham and his seed in the Earlier Letters

Earlier, on page 53, we set out the following three time periods of the New Testament:

1. The Gospel Period
2. The Acts Period
3. The Post Acts Period

We have seen how both Abraham and his seed have a dominant role in both the Gospel Period and in the Acts of the Apostles. In this chapter we shall consider the position they hold in those letters written during the time covered by the Acts of the Apostles. We shall look first at what these letters say about Abraham, after which we shall look at the Seed of Abraham. Unsurprisingly, there is a consistency between the teaching in the epistles written during the Acts Period and that in the Acts of the Apostles itself. However, the epistles, especially Paul's letter to the Romans, provide a more detailed exposition of the relative positions of Jewish and Gentile believers at this time.

The letters written at this time comprise:

- *Letters to Jews by various writers*:
  Hebrews, 1 & 2 Peter,
  1, 2 & 3 John, Jude and Revelation.

- *Letters to Jews and Gentiles written by Paul*:
  Romans, 1 & 2 Corinthians, Galatians, 1 & 2 Thessalonians.

Abraham in the letters written during the Acts Period

As mentioned in the previous chapter, there were 34 references to Abraham in the four Gospels and 8 in the Acts of the Apostles. However, there are 32 references in the earlier letters - 13 in the letters to Jews and 19 in Paul's earlier letters. Some of these make it very clear that Abraham and his seed are still prominent and had not been cast aside at the cross. For example, when writing to the Romans from Corinth on his third missionary journey, Paul asked:

> Did God reject his people? By no means! I am an Israelite myself, a descendant of Abraham, from the tribe of Benjamin. God did not reject his people, whom he foreknew. (Romans 11:1-2)

And Hebrews indicates that God was still helping the seed of Abraham.

> For surely it is not angels he helps, but Abraham's descendants. (Hebrews 2:16)

And Paul was keen to show to the church at Corinth that he was descended from Abraham and was his seed.

> Are they Hebrews? So am I. Are they Israelites? So am I. Are they Abraham's descendants? So am I. (2 Corinthians 11:22)

There are two long passages (Romans 4:1-25 and Galatians 3:6-18) where Abraham is central in the argument that people are saved by grace through faith and that circumcision and keeping the Law has no part to play in salvation. Both passages are well worth reading but the major points are that:

- Abraham believed God and it was credited to Him as righteousness. (Galatians 3:6 and Romans 4:3,9 referring to Genesis 15:6.)
- This was 430 years before the Law was given. (Galatians 3:17)
- And it was also before Abraham was circumcised. (Romans 4:10)

Thus keeping the Law and rituals, such as circumcision, can have no part in having righteousness credited by God.

Abraham is also put forward as the great example of how true faith manifests itself in works.

James makes this clear.

> You foolish man, do you want evidence that faith without deed is useless [dead]. Was not our ancestor Abraham considered righteous for what he did when he offered his son Isaac on the altar? You see that his faith and his actions were working together, and his faith was made complete by what he did. And the scripture was fulfilled that says, "Abraham believed God, and it was credited to him as righteousness," and he was called God's friend. (James 2:20-23)

Hebrews also refers to the faithfulness of Abraham in various matters. For example:

- When called to leave Ur, he obeyed and went.
- When told, in his old age, he was to be a father, he believed.
- When told to offer Isaac, he was prepared to do so. (See Hebrews 11:8-12; 17-19 for details.)

There are a number of other references to Abraham in these earlier letters. For example:

- In Hebrews 6:13-14, when God promised him a child in his old age, God swore by His own name;

- Hebrews 7:1-10 refers to Abraham meeting Melchizedek;

- Sarah is referred to as Abraham's wife in 1 Peter 3:5-6; and

- In both Romans 9:7-9 and Galatians 4:22-23 there are references to Ishmael, the child of Abraham by Hagar, and to Isaac, the child of promise, Abraham had by Sarah.

In all this we can see that the person of Abraham was still significant in the earlier letters, but what about his descendants, the people of Israel – the seed of Abraham?

Letters to the seed of Abraham (i.e. the Jews)

First of all we should note that although six of the fifteen letters written during this time period were written by Paul to mixed congregations of Jews and Gentiles, the other nine were written to Jews. A little attention to the detail in these letters shows this to be the case. For example:

- James addressed his letter to "The twelve tribes scattered abroad" (James 1:1). The word for 'scattered' is *diaspora*, a term used for the 'dispersed' of Israel, those scattered throughout the Roman Empire and beyond.

- Peter wrote his two letters to the same group of people: "To God's elect, strangers in the world, scattered *(diaspora)* throughout ..." (1 Peter 1:1; see also 2 Peter 3:1, which states that this was the second letter he was writing to them.)

- John, in his first of three letters wrote, "He [Christ] is the atoning sacrifice for our sins, and not only for ours but also for the sins of the whole world" (1 John 2:2). The 'our' refers to his people, the Jews, the people he is writing to, and here we see they have first place and the (Gentile) world has second place. This is the situation we saw in the previous chapter when considering the Acts of the Apostles, and we shall see it again, later in this chapter, when we look at some of Paul's earlier letters.

It is not surprising that James, Peter and John wrote to the people of Israel. As indicated on page 75, these three made an agreement with Paul and Barnabas when they met in Jerusalem:

> James, Peter and John, those reputed to be pillars, gave me and Barnabas the right hand of fellowship when they recognised the grace given to me. They agreed that we should go to the Gentiles [nations], and they to the Jews. (Galatians 2:9)

As for the other three letters:

- Hebrews, by its title and content, is very much a letter for the Christian Jews. The Gentile Christians of the Acts Period would have had difficulty following many of its arguments until they had gained a good knowledge of the Old Testament, and especially the Pentateuch (the first five books of the Old Testament).

- Jude was again written to a Jewish Christian congregation. It includes references to apocryphal Jewish writings such as *The Book of Enoch* and *The Assumption of Moses*, which few Gentiles would have read, and many of whom would not even have heard of.

- Revelation[7], with its heavy dependence upon a knowledge and understanding of the Old Testament prophecies, would have

---

[7] We have classed Revelation as a 'letter' since it includes the letters to the Seven Churches in Asia: see Revelation chapters 2 and 3.

been incomprehensible to the new Gentile Christians of the first century. They needed to gain a good knowledge of such books as Daniel and Zechariah before they could start to gain an understanding of Revelation.

An overview of the earlier letters

The table on page 67 compared the occurrences of terms relating to Abraham in the Gospels and the Acts of the Apostles. If we now extend this table to include the letters written during the Acts Period we find the following:

	The Gospels	The Acts of the Apostles	Letters to Jews	Paul's Earlier Letters
	89 chapters	28 chapters	59 chapters	59 chapters
Abraham	34	8	13	19
Israel / Israelite	31	21	6	17
Jew / Jews / Jewish	72	81	2	29
Jerusalem	66	61	4	10

It is interesting to note that terms pertaining to the seed of Abraham in the letters to Jews have a lower frequency than in the other groupings. However, as mentioned above, those letters were addressed to Jews, who were well-versed in the Scriptures. There was therefore not as much need to go into detail as there was in Paul's letters. His earlier letters were addressed to Christian congregations comprising not only Jews but also

Gentiles. As a result, his writings can be a little more difficult to fathom out in places, as we have to decide whether he is addressing the Jewish or Gentile elements in the churches, or both.

The New Covenant[8]

This was a covenant promised to the house of Israel and the house of Judah in the Old Testament (Jeremiah 31:31). In 2 Corinthians 3:5-6, we read:

> Not that we are competent in ourselves to claim anything for ourselves, but our competence comes from God. He has made us competent as ministers of a new covenant ...

As mentioned on pages 48-50, Jeremiah clearly stated that this new covenant was with Israel and Judah and so this statement of Paul clearly shows that the seed of Abraham were still very much a part of God's purpose. However, the new covenant had not yet come in, as Hebrews makes clear:

> By calling this covenant "new," he has made the first one obsolete; and what is obsolete and ageing will soon disappear. (Hebrews 8:13)

So did the old covenant become obsolete and disappear? And did the new covenant come in?

> "The time is coming", declares the Lord, "when I will make a new covenant with the house of Israel and with the house of Judah. It will not be like the covenant I made with their forefathers when I took them by the hand to lead them out of Egypt, because they did not remain faithful to my covenant, and I turned away from them," declares the Lord.

---

[8] For more on the New Covenant see page 139.

"This is the covenant I will make with the house of Israel after that time, declares the Lord. I will put my laws in their minds and write them on their hearts. I will be their God, and they will be my people.

No longer will a man teach his neighbour, or a man his brother, saying, 'Know the Lord,' because they *will all know me*, from the least of them to the greatest. For I will forgive their wickedness and will remember their sins no more." (Hebrews 8:8-12)

Here we see Jeremiah 31:31-34 repeated in detail.

Some suggest that the new covenant came in at the Cross and that we, today, are under the new covenant. That is because we are saved by grace through faith, and the new covenant is a covenant of grace. Such views tend to concentrate on the last verse which states that "I will forgive their wickedness and will remember their sins no more." However, they ignore the other aspects of the new covenant such as that it was made with "the house of Israel and the house of Judah", and Romans 9:4 tells us that the covenants, as well as the Law, belong to Israel.

Also when the new covenant is in operation, it will be a time when the Law is to be written on Israel's minds and upon their hearts, and it will be a time when all Israel will be saved because "they will all know me".

Paul and the other Apostles were ministers of 'the new covenant' in the sense that they taught that if Israel repented Christ would come back, and restore all things (Acts 3:9-21). Then He would set up His kingdom upon earth and Israel would be under the new covenant. This was what they hoped for at that time, and this is why the majority of those letters written during the Acts Period talk about it being the last times and that Christ was expected to return soon.

Hebrews was written at that time, so when it was written the new covenant was still being held out to the people of Israel and Judah. However, it had clearly not come in and never has since.

The relationship between Jewish and Gentile believers – "First to the Jew"

In chapter 6, we noted the changes that took place as Acts progressed. The message of the risen Lord Jesus was initially preached exclusively to Jews but gradually Gentiles (starting with Cornelius and other "God-fearers") were evangelised. As the Gospel spread, other Gentiles, who had no prior connection with Judaism (such as those at Athens, Philippi and Ephesus) were brought into the church. What exactly was the Lord's purpose in doing this and what was the relationship between these Gentile converts and the physical descendants of Abraham – the Jewish believers?

When Paul met Christ on the Damascus road, the Lord gave him a commission:

> "This man is my chosen instrument to proclaim my name *to the Gentiles* and their kings and *to the people of Israel.*" (Acts 9:15)

Paul, then, was given a dual ministry at his conversion – to Jews and to Gentiles – and he explains the relationship between these two groups in his letter to the Romans. This is believed to be the last of the letters he wrote during the Acts Period.

In Romans 1:16 we read:

> For I am not ashamed of the gospel, because it is the power of God that brings salvation to everyone who believes: *first for the Jew*, then for the Gentile.

Here he wrote that the gospel of salvation was first for the Jew and, as we saw in the previous chapter, on his missionary journeys, in any new city, Paul always went first to the synagogue of the Jews. He did so on the first Sabbath he was in Pisidian Antioch. On the second Sabbath many turned up to hear Paul.

When the *Jews* saw the crowds, *they* were filled with jealousy. *They* began to contradict what Paul was saying and heaped abuse on him. Then Paul and Barnabas answered *them* boldly: "*We had to speak the word of God to you first.* Since *you* reject it and do not consider yourselves worthy of eternal life, we now turn to the *Gentiles.*" (Acts 13:45-46)

So during the Acts Period the Jews were to hear the gospel first, but that was not the only issue in which they held first place.

There will be trouble and distress for every human being who does evil: *first for the Jew,* then for the Gentile; but glory, honour and peace for everyone who does good: *first for the Jew,* then for the Gentile. (Romans 2:9-10)

Now it may not be very clear to us what Paul was referring to by 'trouble and distress' and by 'glory, honour and peace'. As for the 'trouble and distress', certainly the Jewish Christians suffered persecution before the Gentile Christians. As mentioned in the previous chapter, the persecution we see in the New Testament is that of Jewish Christians, mainly by the Jewish leadership. The persecution at the hands of the Romans (which was mainly persecution of Gentile Christians) did not commence until the latter part of Nero's reign (about AD 64; which is after the end of the Acts Period). Also we read of judgements from God falling upon such Jews as Ananias and Sapphira, King Herod and Elymas (Acts 5:1-10; 12:21-23; 13:6-12), and it is interesting to note that there is no record in the New Testament of any such divine judgments falling upon Gentiles.

As for the 'glory, honour and peace', in Acts we do see the Jews benefitting from such blessings as healing before any Gentiles did so, and the Jews of the Acts Period did have the honour of being the leaders. In fact there is no record of any Gentiles having a leadership position during the time covered by the Acts of the Apostles. But however we understand Romans 2:9-10, these verses show clearly that the Jew was first. In fact at that time, there were very many advantages in being a Jew, as Paul makes clear.

What *advantage*, then, is there *in being a Jew*, or what value is there in circumcision? *Much in every way!* First of all, the Jews have been entrusted with the very words of God.
(Romans 3:1-2)

Israel's hardening in part

In the previous chapter, it was suggested that the events in Acts indicate that Israel had not been rejected at the cross. On the contrary, there was much advantage in every way in being a Jew. Paul deals with this issue in depth in Romans 11 and it is worth examining his argument. First, he refutes the suggestion that Israel had been rejected.

I ask then: did God reject his people? By no means! I am an Israelite myself, a descendant of Abraham, from the tribe of Benjamin. *God did **not** reject his people*, whom he foreknew. (Romans 11:1-2)

Thus when Romans was written (from Corinth on Paul's third missionary journey, Acts 20:2-3) the seed of Abraham had not been rejected by God, but were still in the forefront of His purposes for mankind. However, the situation was far from healthy. The Jewish leadership had rejected Christ, persecuted Him and executed Him; now they were rejecting the preaching of the Apostles, and were mistreating them and other Jewish Christians. In Romans 11 Paul describes this situation in terms of a *partial* hardening and a *partial* blindness:

Again I ask: did they [Israel] stumble so as to fall beyond recovery? Not at all. (Romans 11:11)

I do not want you to be ignorant of this mystery, brothers, so that you may not be conceited: Israel has experienced a *hardening in part* ... (Romans 11:25)

> For I would not, brethren, that ye should be ignorant of this
> mystery, lest ye should be wise in your own conceits; that
> *blindness in part* is happened to Israel ... (Romans 11:25, *KJV*)

So although Israel held first place, the nation had stumbled (but not
beyond recovery); they were partially blind, but had not yet lost all sight;
they had hardened their hearts, but not totally. What could help them
regain their balance and sight? What could help them soften their hearts?
This was where the Gentiles of the Acts Period came in.

> Again I ask: Did they stumble so as to fall beyond recovery? Not
> at all! Rather, because of their transgression, salvation has come
> to the Gentiles *to make Israel envious.* But if their transgression
> means riches for the world, and their loss means riches for the
> Gentiles, how much greater riches will their fullness bring! I am
> talking to you Gentiles. Inasmuch as I am the apostle to the
> Gentiles, I make much of my ministry *in the hope that I may
> somehow arouse my own people to envy and save some of them.*
> (Romans 11:11-14)

The purpose of God was for Israel to be saved, to become a kingdom of
priests and to take the message of Christ out to the Gentile world and, in
doing so, bring the promises made to Abraham to fruition. However, that
nation was stumbling and failing to take their place in God's purposes.
What could help them recover? We are told that salvation had come to
the Gentiles to make Israel envious ... to arouse Israel to envy ... and so
save some of them. That was the reason God had turned to the Gentiles
during the Acts Period. But did the strategy work?

Israel provoked to 'envy'

We often look at the word 'envy' and see only its negative connotations.
We may see someone who has a better car than us, envy them, and take
a dislike to them. Or may have superior skills to us and, again, we may
envy them and have negative feelings about them. However, some people
may be motivated by that envy, to work harder to earn money for that

car, or to practise a skill that another may have and so become better at it. It is this positive sense of 'envy' that is the focus in this passage in Romans, and this is brought out in some translations. For example:

> For I speak to you Gentiles, inasmuch as I am the apostle of the Gentiles, I magnify mine office: If by any means I may provoke to *emulation* them which are my flesh, and might save some of them. (Romans 11:13-14, *KJV*)

Here the *KJV* has 'emulation', rather than 'envy', and to 'emulate' means to imitate, to follow (*Amplified Bible*). God wanted the Jews to 'imitate' those Gentiles who had come to believe in Christ.

Later in the chapter, Paul describes how this might happen with an illustration from olive farming. Olive trees may live for hundreds of years, in some cases over a thousand. As they grow old the fruit becomes smaller, with less flesh. If that tree is cut down and a new one planted, it can take fifty or more years before it bears any significant fruit. Olive farming had developed a technique to stimulate an old tree into bearing more good fruit. An old branch or two were cut off, and branches of a wild olive tree were grafted in. The vigour from the wild olive would invigorate the old tree into bearing more and better olives.

The olive tree of Israel

In the Old Testament, the olive tree was used extensively by the Israelites in their religious life; the cherubim of Solomon's temple were made from olive wood (1 Kings 6:23) and in Judges 9:8 it is called the king of trees. It came to be symbolic of the nation of Israel itself. In Romans 11, Paul picks up the picture of Israel as a cultivated olive tree. Addressing Gentile believers in Romans 11:17, Paul says:

> If some of the branches have been broken off, and you, though a wild olive shoot, have been grafted in among the others and now share in the nourishing sap from the olive root ...

To what was he referring here? Clearly, from Romans, the people of Israel still occupied first place in God's purpose for mankind. Unfortunately the nation had stumbled because some of the Jews had hardened their hearts against the person of Christ and the Apostles' message that He was their Messiah, the Son of God and the Saviour. These were the branches that had been broken off. However, when the message was taken to the Gentiles, some of them believed in Christ as their Saviour, and these were the branches that had been grafted in. In God's view the Gentiles of the Acts Period, those who had placed their faith in Christ as their Saviour, were considered Abraham's seed.

> There is neither Jew nor Greek, slave nor free, male nor female, for you are all one in Christ Jesus. If you belong to Christ, then you are Abraham's seed, and heirs according to the promise. (Galatians 3:28-29)

> Therefore, the promise comes by faith, so that it may be by grace and may be guaranteed to all Abraham's offspring - not only to those who are of the law but also to those who are of the faith of Abraham. He is the father of us all. As it is written: "I have made you a father of many nations." (Romans 4:16-17)

For Gentiles to be looked upon as Abraham's offspring, to be considered his seed, without being circumcised and purely on the basis of their faith in Christ, should, indeed, have made Israel envious.

But would the salvation of the Gentiles (the wild olive branches) stimulate the people of Israel (the cultivated olive tree) into bearing fruit? Would the Gentiles provoke Israel into envy / emulation, and so save some? Did it work?

> I do not want you to be ignorant of this mystery, brothers, so that you may not be conceited: Israel has experienced a hardening in part until the full number of the Gentiles has come in. And so all Israel will be saved ... (Romans 11:25-26)

Romans 11:26 talks about 'the full number' of Gentiles coming in. In terms of the figure of the olive tree ... how many wild olive branches would it take to stimulate a cultivated olive tree into bearing good fruit? And what would happen if too many wild olive branches were grafted in? The answer to the first question is uncertain, but the answer to the second is that the tree would become useless; any fruit borne would, in effect, be small, bitter, wild olives. The tree would be cut down.

So from Acts 10 onwards, when the first Gentile Cornelius was grafted in, this was the situation throughout the remainder of the Acts Period. As we have said, Romans was written from Corinth when Paul was there for three months (Acts 20:1-2). However, after he had written it, we find in the last third of Acts that the descendants of Abraham were still in prime position.

Paul told Agrippa:

> "And now it is because of my hope in what God has *promised our fathers* that I am on trial today. This is the *promise* our *twelve tribes* are hoping to see fulfilled as they earnestly serve God day and night." (Acts 26:6-7)

Note again that Paul refers to:

- 'our fathers' (namely Abraham, Isaac and Jacob);
- the 'twelve tribes'; and
- the 'promise' made to the fathers, that the twelve tribes would be a nation, have a land, be blessed and be a blessing to other (Gentile) nations.

When Paul reached Rome, he called the *leaders of the Jews* together (Acts 28:17). He spoke to them about the *hope of Israel* and tried to convince those Jewish leaders, from the Law of Moses and from the Prophets about Jesus (Acts 28:20,23). As usual some believed and some did not, and Paul was moved to quote from Isaiah's judgmental prophecy.

The original prophecy resulted in Israel being conquered, the temple and city destroyed, and the people being taken into captivity by the Babylonians. Could something like that happen again?

Things come to a head

Before answering that question, perhaps we should ask why things had come to a head with the people of Israel. After all, as mentioned in the previous chapter, from Pentecost in Acts 2 there had been an undercurrent of opposition from the Jewish leadership, who arrested Peter and John, imprisoned them and flogged them. Stephen was stoned and great persecution broke out against the church in Jerusalem (Acts 8:1). James was killed by Herod and Peter imprisoned (Acts 12:1-4). Paul was abused by the Jews at Pisidian Antioch (Acts 13:45); he was stoned by Jews from Antioch and Iconium (Acts 14:19); and so it went on. On his last visit to Jerusalem he had to be rescued from the Jews by the Roman commander (Acts 21:30-32). So what had brought things to a head?

About the time Paul arrived in Rome something very significant happened in Jerusalem. We read of Ananus, the high priest in the temple in Jerusalem.

> But this younger Ananus, who, as we have already told you took the high priesthood, was a bold man in his temper, and very insolent; he was also of the sect of the Sadducees, who were very rigid in judging offenders, above all the rest of the Jews, as we have already observed; when, therefore, Ananus was of this disposition, he thought he had now a proper opportunity [to exercise his authority]. Festus was now dead, and Albinus was but upon the road; so he assembled the Sanhedrin of judges and brought before them the brother of Jesus, who was called the Christ, whose name was James, and some others, [or some of his companions;] and when he had formed an accusation against them as breakers of the law, he delivered them to be stoned ... (Josephus; *Antiquities of the Jews*, 20,9,1)

Festus, the governor we read about in Acts 25, suddenly died and during the hiatus before the next governor, Albinus, arrived, Ananus took the opportunity to execute James and many other Jewish Christians in Jerusalem. The previous generation of Jewish leaders had rejected Jesus and had Him crucified. This generation of Jewish leaders now rejected the brother of Jesus, and had him stoned. The 'cup of iniquity' was full and so, for the final time in the New Testament, Isaiah's judgemental prophecy is quoted.

> "'Go to this people and say,
> 'You will be ever hearing but never understanding;
>   you will be ever seeing but never perceiving.'
> For this people's *heart has become calloused;*
>   they hardly hear with their ears,
>   and they have closed their eyes.
> Otherwise they might see with their eyes,
>   hear with their ears,
>   understand with their hearts
> and turn, and I would heal them."
> (Acts 28:26-27; quoting from Isaiah 6[9])

The situation we read about in Romans 11 had deteriorated. By the end of Acts the nation had stumbled beyond recovery; the partial blindness and hardness of heart had become total and, similar to Isaiah's time, the people of Israel were judged, not by the Babylonians, but by the Romans. They, like the Babylonians, destroyed Jerusalem and the temple, and exiled those Jews who were not killed to the far reaches of the Roman Empire.

What happened to the Gentiles?

After pronouncing Isaiah's prophecy to the Jewish leaders in Rome, Paul then told them:

---

[9] For more on Isaiah 6 and its use in Acts 28, see page 134.

"Therefore I want you to know that God's salvation has been sent to the Gentiles, *and they will listen!"* (Acts 28:28)

Unlike the Jews, Paul said the Gentiles would listen, but the Gentiles had been grafted into the olive tree of Israel. They shared in Israel's blessings; they were considered, along with Israel, to be the seed of Abraham; his offspring. However, if that tree was no longer viable; if, in the terms of Isaiah, it was now a stump, what happened to the Gentile branches?
To answer that question, and see the significance of the statement "God's salvation has been sent to the Gentiles, and they will listen", we will need to look at what happened next. We are told:

> For two whole years Paul stayed there in his own rented house and welcomed all who came to see him. (Acts 28:30)

During those two years he wrote Ephesians, Philippians, Colossians and Philemon, and a little later 1 and 2 Timothy and Titus. It is from these letters that we will learn about the seed of Abraham and the Gentiles in the Post Acts Period.

Abraham and his seed   101

Chapter 8

Abraham and his seed in Paul's Later Letters

Progressive revelation

So far we have traced the progressive revelation about Abraham and his seed through the Old and New Testaments. These were the people whom God had called out and covenanted with and whom He was going to bless, not solely for their own sakes but so that they might be a means of blessing to the whole earth.

But who were this group? The Lord Jesus, for example in John 8:39-47, suggested that not all the natural descendants of Abraham are the true "seed of Abraham." He accused the Jews of being the children of the devil (John 8:44) because if they had really been Abraham's children they would have listened to Him (John 8:39). Paul also, in Romans 9:6-8, made this point:

> … not all who are descended from Israel are Israel. Nor because they are his descendants are they all Abraham's children. On the contrary, "It is through Isaac that your offspring will be reckoned." In other words, it is not the natural descendants who are God's children, but it is the children of the promise who are regarded as Abraham's offspring.

However, in writing to the Galatians, a church comprising both Jews and Gentiles, Paul went further and suggested that some people who were *not* natural descendants (Gentiles) *were* included in the group.

The criterion for membership was faith in Christ. So as Paul says to the Galatians:

> If you belong to Christ, then you are Abraham's seed and heirs according to the promise. (Galatians 3:29)

But the conclusion of Galatians 3:29 is expanded in Romans 11 (as discussed in chapter 7), where Paul explains the relative positions of Jews and Gentile believers in the seed of Abraham. Paul sums up the situation of Israel in the Acts Period in Romans 11:25:

> Israel has experienced a hardening in part until the full number of the Gentiles has come in.

The olive tree revisited

In Paul's analogy of the olive tree the "natural" (Jewish) branches of the tree had been cut off and "wild" olive branches grafted in to stimulate the tree to life again. That was the reason at that time for bringing the Gospel to the Gentiles.

Paul then goes on to express the hope that Israel would respond and raises the bizarre possibility (from a gardening perspective) that the natural branches that had been cut off might one day be grafted back in. He finishes his argument by saying:

> After all, if *you* were cut out of an olive tree that is *wild by nature*, and contrary to nature were grafted in to a *cultivated olive tree*, how much more readily will these, the *natural branches*, be grafted into their *own olive tree*. (Romans 11:24)

So Gentile Christians were being brought into something that belonged to Israel. The Israelites were the natural descendants of Abraham, the natural branches. Those who rejected Jesus as the Christ, the Son of God, were cut off and the Gentiles who believed but who were not natural descendants of Abraham (wild branches), were brought into that group "contrary to nature." But these Gentiles were essentially being brought into the community of saved Israel. And the reason for bringing the Gentiles in was to provoke Israel to respond.

So did this strategy work? Unfortunately the last two millennia reveal that Israel has not turned to the Lord Jesus. So is this process of grafting in wild branches to provoke Israel still continuing today, even though for 1,900 of these 2,000 years Israel has not existed as a nation?

In Acts 28 we read of Paul's judgment on the Jewish leaders in Rome, where he quotes the indictment from Isaiah 6 that they would not listen (see page 100). Paul concludes by stating that God's salvation has been sent to the Gentiles and they *will* listen.

But what was new about that? The message had been going to Gentiles since Cornelius in Acts 10. Or was this something different?

During the book of Acts, the leaders of the local churches that were springing up were virtually all Jewish but by the end of the first century AD that had all changed. Gentiles began to be responsible for the churches and by early in the second century AD early church history shows that church leadership had shifted to Gentile Christians.

So was this just a natural, slow trend or was there some kind of seismic shift that took place after Paul's pronouncement of the rejection of Israel in Acts 28?

Paul's later writings

After the end of Acts Paul wrote seven letters – Ephesians, Philippians, Colossians, Philemon, 1 & 2 Timothy and Titus. There is some debate about the *exact* date that these letters were written but it is generally accepted that it was during the 60s AD. Ephesians, Colossians and Philemon written together during Paul's two year imprisonment in Rome. Philippians was also written about the same time. 1 Timothy and Titus were written during a period when Paul was freed after the two years and

2 Timothy was written from a second period of imprisonment at the end of which Paul was executed.

In the New Testament, Abraham is one of the most frequently mentioned Old Testament characters. But in these seven letters there is *not one* reference to him at all, compared with 19 references in Paul's earlier letters. Not only so, but when we include other words relating to Abraham and his seed – the Israelites – the contrast becomes even more apparent. The table below shows the number of references to particular words in each group of seven letters.

Occurrences of words relating to Abraham in Paul's writings

	Paul's Six Earlier Letters	Paul's Seven Later Letters
	59 chapters	28 chapters
Abraham	19	0
Isaac, Jacob	5	0
Israel/Israelite	17	2
Jew/Jews/Jewish	29	2
Circumcis (e)(ed) (ion) (ing)	32	9
Moses	9	1
Total	111	14

Notwithstanding the difference in size between the two sections, the change in emphasis is quite striking, especially when we consider the context of the usage of these terms in the later letters. The 14 occurrences of each of these key words in the later letters are as follows:

Israel/Israelite

Ephesians 2:12-13

> ... remember that at that time you were separate from Christ, excluded from citizenship in **Israel** and foreigners to the covenants of promise, without hope and without God in the world. But now in Christ Jesus you who once were far away have been brought near through the blood of Christ.

Here Paul is explaining the position of Gentiles *in the past*, in contrast to their present position. They *were* excluded but now they have now been brought near to God by the blood of Christ.

Philippians 3:5

> ... circumcised on the eighth day, of the people of **Israel**, of the tribe of Benjamin, a Hebrew of Hebrews.

This is part of Paul's description of his *past*, which he was prepared to consider loss for the sake of Christ (Philippians 3:7).

Jew/Jews/Jewish

Colossians 3:11

> Here there is no Greek or **Jew**, circumcised or uncircumcised, barbarian, Scythian, slave or free, but Christ is all and is in all.

In the church which is the body of Christ, old distinctions disappear. Christ is all.

Titus 1:14

> … rebuke them sharply, so that they will be sound in the faith and will pay no attention to **Jewish** myths or to the commands of those who reject the truth.

Paul is urging Titus, who was in charge of the church in Crete, to eliminate false teaching from the church, including "Jewish myths."

Circumcis (e) (ed) (ion) (ing)

Philippians 3:5

> … **circumcised** on the eighth day, of the people of Israel, of the tribe of Benjamin, a Hebrew of Hebrews.

Again, this is part of Paul's description of his *past*, which he was prepared to consider loss for the sake of Christ (Philippians 3:7).

Colossians 2:11(3 occurrences)

> In him you were also **circumcised**, in the putting off of the sinful nature, not with a **circumcision** done by the hands of men, but with the **circumcision** done by Christ.

In this verse, Paul contrasts physical circumcision done by men with the "circumcision" of the heart accomplished by Christ in the believer.

Ephesians 2:11

> Therefore, remember that formerly you who are Gentiles by birth and called "uncircumcised" by those who call themselves "the **circumcision**" (that done in the body by the hands of men)…

Again Paul is speaking of the *past* condition of Gentiles, as "uncircumcised," in a physical sense, as an introduction to what he is about to say in Ephesians 2:13:

> *But now* in Christ Jesus you who once were far away have been brought near through the blood of Christ.

Philippians 3:2-3

> Watch out for those dogs, those men who do evil, those mutilators of the flesh. For it is we who are the **circumcision**, we who worship by the Spirit of God, who glory in Christ Jesus and who put no confidence in the flesh.

Here Paul is speaking of the "true" circumcision that Christ accomplishes in the believer, who does not trust in the flesh. This is contrasted with the physical circumcision and the other hallmarks of racial superiority that characterised Paul's past life as a Pharisee (see above under Israel/Israelite), which he is about to describe in the following verses of Philippians 3. It is worth noting his description of those who prided themselves in their physical circumcision as "dogs" and "mutilators of the flesh." This shows how strongly he felt about the dangers of focusing on racial or physical "superiority."

Colossians 3:11

> Here there is no Greek or Jew, **circumcised** or uncircumcised, barbarian, Scythian, slave or free, but Christ is all and is in all.

All men and women, irrespective of their pedigree, are one in Christ, who is all and in all.

Colossians 4:11

> Jesus, who is called Justus, also sends greetings. These are the only **Jews (Greek: "of the circumcision")** among my fellow workers for the kingdom of God.

Even by the time Paul wrote Colossians, the majority of Christian workers appear to have been non-Jews.

Titus 1:10

> For there are many rebellious people, mere talkers and deceivers, especially those of the **circumcision** group.

During the Acts Period, the question of whether Gentiles needed to be circumcised dogged the apostles. The Jerusalem Council, described in Acts 15, dealt with this issue and confirmed that Gentiles were not required to keep the Law. Now, some 15 years later, Titus obviously was encountering similar problems in Crete and Paul was ordering him to stamp out this heresy.

Moses

2 Timothy 3:8

> Just as Jannes and Jambres opposed **Moses**, so also these men oppose the truth.

Here we have a *historic* reference to Pharaoh's magicians, who opposed Moses in Egypt. The men who contested with Timothy as a church leader, were similar to these magicians in their opposition to the truth. Timothy, who had a Jewish mother, would understand the reference.

When we examine these references to Abraham and other terms related to Israel in the last seven letters we find that they are either:

- historic references,
- stated to contrast the present situation with the past, or
- used to describe a particular type of opposition that the church leaders were facing.

The context in which the message of Christ was now being presented was independent of its historic links with Abraham. And the reason for this was that Paul had received a new revelation of a "mystery" that had previously been hidden.

The revelation of the mystery

Addressing "you Gentiles" (Ephesians 3:1) Paul explains this revelation:

> Surely you have heard about the administration of God's grace that was given to me for you, that is, the mystery made known to me by revelation, as I have already written briefly. In reading this, then, you will be able to understand my insight into the mystery of Christ, which was not made known to men in other generations as it has now been revealed by the Spirit to God's holy apostles and prophets. (Ephesians 3:2-5)

In this paragraph Paul speaks of two "mysteries." The first is simply called "the mystery" and it was made known to Paul by revelation. This mystery had *never before been revealed* (see also Ephesians 3:9 and Colossians 1:26). By reading what Paul has to say about this, the readers will obtain an understanding of Paul's insight into the "mystery of Christ," which had been made known to previous generations but not *as it has now been revealed.*

Unlike "the mystery", the mystery of Christ *had* been revealed progressively throughout Scripture. For example:

- Abraham rejoiced at the thought of seeing the day of the Lord Jesus Christ (John 8:56).

- David spoke of the resurrection of the Christ (Acts 2:31).
- The prophets predicted the coming of Christ (e.g. Isaiah 42:1-4, Matthew 12:17-21).

But this new revelation of "the mystery of Christ" was now on a different basis from previous revelations, because it reveals Him as head of the church which is His body.

So what does Paul mean by "the mystery," which gives fresh insight into this new dimension of the "mystery of Christ"?

"The mystery" in Ephesians and Colossians relates to the uniting of believing Jews and believing Gentiles into one "body:"

> This mystery (i.e. "the mystery") is that through the gospel the Gentiles are heirs together with Israel, members together of one body, and sharers together in the promise in Christ Jesus. (Ephesians 3:6)

In the NIV translation quoted above, the words "with Israel" have been inserted by the English translators. They are not in the original Greek and actually miss the point that Paul is trying to make. Other translations capture Paul's meaning more accurately. For example:

> ... that the Gentiles should be fellowheirs, and of the same body, and partakers of his promise in Christ by the gospel (KJV)

> ... that in Christ Jesus the Gentiles are co-heirs, companions and co-partners in the Promise. (Moffatt)

It is literally that the believers in all the nations are joint-heirs and a joint body and joint-sharers of the promise in Christ. Some writers have even suggested that Paul invented the word "joint body" to suit his purposes here. The point is that there are no longer any differences between Jewish and Gentile Christians. They are all treated equally as one, not by

Gentiles joining themselves to Israel's blessings, as it was in the past, but by the formation of a new group – the church which is His body, with Christ as the Head.

Paul then goes on to explain this secret in more detail.

> Although I am less than the least of all God's people, this grace was given to me: to preach to the Gentiles the unsearchable riches of Christ, and to make plain to everyone the administration of this mystery, which for ages past was kept hidden in God, who created all things.
> (Ephesians 3:8-9)

So this was not a new idea that God had introduced out of the blue. This was His plan all along. But for ages past it had been kept hidden – only at this time was it being revealed.

But Ephesians is not the only place where this is mentioned. In Colossians 1:25-27 Paul says:

> I have become its (the church's) servant by the commission God gave me to present to you the word of God in its fullness – the mystery that has been kept hidden for ages and generations, but is *now* disclosed to the saints. To them God has chosen to make known among the Gentiles the glorious riches of this mystery, which is Christ in you, the hope of glory.

The mystery, which had been hidden in ages past, is Christ in you Gentiles, the hope of glory.

Sometime previously, when Paul stood before Agrippa, he said:

> It is because of my hope in what God has promised our fathers that I am on trial today. This is **the promise our twelve tribes are hoping to see fulfilled** as they earnestly serve God day and night. (Acts 26:6-7)

I am saying **nothing beyond what the prophets and Moses said would happen** – that the Christ would suffer and, as the first to rise from the dead, would proclaim light to his own people and to the Gentiles. (Acts 26:22-23)

That resonates with what Paul wrote in Galatians and Romans, but it does not sit well with the statement in Ephesians 3:4-5 and Colossians 1:26 that this mystery was something that had *not* been revealed previously.

As Sherring observes:

> … this dispensation was not revealed until the later ministry of Paul. There is nothing in the Old Testament, Gospels, Acts or the letters written during the Acts Period, that refers to this administration. It was revealed some time after Paul began his imprisonment in Rome (Acts 28:30,31). (Brian Sherring, *The Mystery of Ephesians*, p38)

Under the revelation of this mystery, the Jew was no longer "first"; Gentile Christians were no longer being brought into a group of believers that were essentially the true Israel; there is no connection between the members of this body and Abraham. All believers, whatever their nationality, are all on an equal footing before God in Christ. They are members of the Body of Christ, with the Lord Jesus as the Head of the Body.

So what are the implications of all this? There are several but we will focus on what Paul's later letters reveal about two aspects of God's purposes:

- The destiny of this joint body of believers – a destiny in the heavenly realms, in contrast to the destiny of the seed of Abraham in the land, and

- The use of the term "fullness" to describe the Lord Jesus and His church in the context of God's ultimate reconciliation of all creation to Himself.

The church's sphere of blessing

When God called Abraham in Genesis 12, He promised him that he would be given a land – the land from the River of Egypt to the River Euphrates – and that his seed (the people of Israel) would become a great nation who would be a means of blessing to all the nations on the earth. Abraham, however, looked beyond the land to the city of God. The letter to the Hebrews tells us that:

> By faith he (Abraham) made his home in the promised land like a stranger in a foreign country... For he was looking forward to the city with foundations, whose architect and builder is God. (Hebrews 11:9-10)

The city, of course, is the new Jerusalem, which we read of in Revelation, coming down from heaven to the new earth:

> I saw the Holy City, the new Jerusalem, coming down out of heaven from God, prepared as a bride beautifully dressed for her husband. And I heard a loud voice from the throne saying, "Now the dwelling of God is with men, and he will live with them. They will be his people and God himself will be with them and be their God." (Revelation 21:2-3)

His descendant David, king of Israel, was promised that his throne would be established forever (2 Samuel 7:16) and the prophets (see e.g. Isaiah 9:7) foretold the coming of the Lord Jesus to fulfil this role. This is also confirmed in the New Testament (see e.g. Luke 1:32-33).

The focus of the future blessing of the seed of Abraham is thus very much linked with the new earth, with David's greater Son ruling from

Jerusalem over the nation and beyond, and God making His dwelling with men. Thus, the promises to Abraham, Isaac and Jacob will be fulfilled – they will be blessed on the earth and also will be a means of blessing to the other nations on the earth.

However, in the opening chapter of Ephesians, we find Paul praising the Lord by saying:

> Praise to the God and Father of our Lord Jesus Christ, who has blessed us **in the heavenly realms** with every spiritual blessing in Christ. (Ephesians 1: 3)

The phrase *en tois epouraniois* ("in the heavenly realms") occurs only in Ephesians. The members of the church which is His body are promised blessings in these "heavenly realms." It has been argued that this does not represent a place but is an attempt to show that these blessings are "spiritual" rather than "physical." However, the same phrase is used to describe the *place* where the risen and glorified Christ is seated at the right hand of God:

> … he raised him from the dead and seated him at his right hand **in the heavenly realms**, far above all rule and authority, power and dominion, and every title that can be given, not only in the present age but also in the one to come. (Ephesians 1:20-21)

This is also the place to which we have been raised with Him:

> And God raised us up with Christ and seated us with him **in the heavenly realms** in Christ Jesus, in order that he might show the incomparable riches of his grace, expressed in his kindness to us in Christ Jesus. (Ephesians 2:6-7)

Here in Ephesians 2, Paul explains that God has raised us up with Christ in the heavenly realms to show "the incomparable riches of his grace." To whom? To the spiritual powers in the heavenly realms. In Ephesians 3, Paul gives us a glimpse of a different dimension of this cosmic purpose:

His intent was that now, through the church the manifold wisdom of God should be made known to the rulers and authorities **in the heavenly realms**, according to his eternal purpose which he accomplished in Christ Jesus our Lord. In him and through faith in him we may approach God with freedom and confidence. (Ephesians 3:10-12)

Some of these "rulers and authorities" in the heavenly realms are hostile to God and His ways, and oppose us:

For our struggle is not against flesh and blood, but against the rulers, against the authorities, against the powers of this dark world and against the spiritual forces of evil **in the heavenly realms**. (Ephesians 6:12)

However, if we wear the full armour of God, as Paul explains in Ephesians 6, we can overcome because the Lord Jesus is already above them. God has seated the Lord Jesus Christ at His right hand in the heavenly realms:

… far above all rule and authority, power and dominion, and every title that can be given, not only in the present age but also in the age to come. And God placed all things under his feet and appointed him to be head over everything for the church, which is his body. (Ephesians 1:21-22)

The revelation of God's eternal purpose in Christ has implications that go far beyond the narrower focus of Abraham and the land. Christ is raised up as head over everything for the church, which is His body. And now all believers – Jew or Gentile – are joint members of this joint body with Him as the Head.

What Paul is saying here is that God's intention was that this church should be raised up to be blessed in the heavenly realms, where Christ is seated, and that through this church He would demonstrate His wisdom to the spiritual beings who live in these heavenly realms.

In Colossians, although the expression "in the heavenly realms" is not used, Paul uses the truth of our destiny there as a basis for encouraging the Colossian believers to live in a way that is appropriate to the position to which God has raised them:

> Since, then, you have been raised with Christ, set your hearts on things above, **where Christ is seated at the right hand of God**. Set your minds on things above, not on earthly things. For you died and your life is now hidden with Christ in God. When Christ, who is your life, appears, then you also will appear with him in glory. (Colossians 3:1-4)

It is hard for us to understand exactly what Paul means by that final sentence. It appears that the Lord Jesus will "appear" in the heavenly places, with His body, the church, possibly before He returns to the earth to establish His kingdom there. However, his words do indicate that the church's sphere of blessing is the heavenly realms, where the Lord Jesus presently is.

Fullness: Bringing things to completion

Paul says in Colossians 1:25 that it was given to him to present the word of God in its **fullness.** The Greek word translated "present ... in its fullness" in Colossians 1:25 comes from the verb *pleroo* = to fill up or complete. It, and its related noun *pleroma* = fullness, appear throughout the New Testament in a variety of everyday settings. For example, they are used in the sense of a net being full of fish (Matthew 13:48), a patch being used to cover a hole in a garment (Matthew 9:16) or even being full of joy (Acts 13:52) or indignation (Acts 5:17). Paul also uses *pleroma* to describe the full number of the Gentiles being brought into Israel's blessings during the Acts Period (Romans 11:12, 25).

However, it is only in his later letters that he uses the term to describe the Lord Jesus Christ, His Church and the climax of the ages. As Paul presents the word of God in its **fullness**, he sets out the Lord Jesus Christ as possessing the **fullness** of the deity, the church being the **fullness** of the Lord Jesus and of God's ultimate purpose of heading up everything in Christ, at some time in the future "when the times will have reached their fulfilment" – literally "the dispensation of the **fullness** of times" (Ephesians 1:10).

The Lord Jesus Christ

In Colossians 1:15,18-20 Paul states that:

> He (Christ) is the image of the invisible God, the firstborn over all creation … And he is the head of the body, the church; he is the beginning and the firstborn from among the dead, so that in everything he might have the supremacy. For God was pleased to have all his **fullness** dwell in him and through him to reconcile to himself all things, whether in heaven or on earth, by making peace through his blood, shed on the cross.

This statement is repeated in Colossians 2:9:

> For in Christ all the **fullness** of the Deity lives in bodily form.

All the complete attributes of the deity dwell in Christ. He is the "image of the invisible God." In the first two chapters of Colossians, Paul sets out the comprehensive nature of Christ's headship:

- He is the firstborn over all creation (Colossians 1:15), not in the sense of being the first to be born but in the sense of being heir. Why so? The next verse explains that this is because everything was created *by* Him and *for* Him.
- He is firstborn from among the dead. He conquered death and became the author of the new creation. As He told His disciples "Because I live, you also will live" (John 14:19).
- As firstborn and heir of both the old and the new creation and, in possession of the full attributes of deity, He is ideally placed to be God's agent for the reconciliation of all things, through His

blood. Every part of the universe – the heavens and the earth, are reconciled to God through Him.

The Church

Having declared in Colossians 2:9 that all the fullness of the Deity lives in bodily form in Christ, Paul immediately goes on to show the implications of this for the members of His body:

> And you have been given **fullness** in Christ, who is head over every power and authority. (Colossians 2:10)

Since the Lord Jesus is seated above all principalities and powers the members of the church which is His body can obtain all we need in Him. This is something that we can find hard to accept because "religion" always finds rites and ceremonies for us to perform thinking they will bring us closer to God. Indeed, Paul goes on to warn his readers against allowing themselves to be judged by others for their religious observances or to be distracted by human religious prohibitions and other practices. He groups these under the heading of "self-imposed worship" (Colossians 2:23).

No, the reality is found in Christ, directly and solely, and we, as members of His body have to maintain our contact with our Head:

> ... from whom the whole body, supported and held together by its ligaments and sinews, grows as God causes it to grow. (Colossians 2:19)

In Ephesians, Paul prays for Christian believers that they will be able to develop their close bond with the Lord. And again, he describes it in terms of fullness:

> I pray that out of his glorious riches he may strengthen you with power through his Spirit in your inner being, so that Christ may dwell in your hearts through faith. And I pray that you, being

rooted and grounded in love, may have power, together with all the saints, to grasp how wide and long and high and deep is the love of Christ, and to know this love that surpasses knowledge – that you may be filled to the measure of all the **fullness** of God. (Ephesians 3:16-19)

What a goal for Christian believers! By allowing Christ to dwell in our hearts we can experience this love that goes beyond knowledge and, ultimately, we can be filled to the measure of the **fullness** of God.

We do not acquire this as individuals, but "together with all the saints." In chapter 4 of Ephesians, Paul develops this further by setting before us the vision of the body of Christ being built up together into complete maturity. The Lord gave gifted individuals to the church, Paul says, but for what purpose?

> … to prepare God's people for works of service, so that the body of Christ may be built up until we all reach unity in the faith and in the knowledge of the Son of God and become mature, attaining to the whole measure of the **fullness** of Christ. (Ephesians 4:12-13)

The church which is the body of Christ has the potential to reach such a level of maturity through our living relationship with Him as our Head.

But there is a further truth to be considered. We have already seen that all the **fullness** of the Godhead dwells in Christ, but the church which is His body is also described as *being* the **fullness** of Christ.

> And God placed all things under his feet and appointed him to be head over everything for the church, which is his body, the **fullness** of him who fills everything in every way. (Ephesians 1:22-23)

In this passage, Christ is the One who "fills everything in every way," and the church is described as the "fullness" of Christ. This could mean that the church is "filled full" by Christ – which is true as it is stated in Colossians 2:10. Alternatively, Paul could be saying that Christ is "filled full" by the church. Both are possible and several commentators warn about the ambiguity of this verse. However elsewhere in the New Testament *pleroma* is almost always used in an active sense, so this passage does indeed appear to be saying that Christ is "filled full" by the church.[10]

This process of filling is still continuing. One day we will stand before Him without spot and blemish, filled to the measure of all the fullness of God (Ephesians 3:19) and attaining to the whole measure of the fullness of Christ (Ephesians 4:13). Only on that day will we be able to be the "fullness of Christ." What a prospect! What condescension for God to bring us into such a position!

The climax of the ages

When will this happen? When will all things in their fullness be brought together? In Ephesians 1, Paul introduces another "mystery" – the mystery of God's will – in particular His purpose to head up everything in Christ.

> And he made known to us the mystery of his will according to his good pleasure, which he purposed in Christ, to be put into effect **when the times will have reached their fulfilment** – to bring all things in heaven and on earth together under one head, even Christ. (Ephesians 1:9-10)

This "dispensation of the **fullness** of times" (KJV) is the time when God will have reconciled all things in heaven and on earth through Christ and will have placed all things under His feet. Christ, in whom all the fullness of the Godhead lives in bodily form, will Himself be filled full by His

---

[10] For a detailed discussion of the meaning of *pleroma* see *That you may be filled* by Charles Ozanne, pp16-17, published by The Open Bible Trust.

body, the church, which will stand, complete in Him in the heavenly realms. All living creatures, in heaven and on earth and under the earth will acknowledge His Lordship and marvel at the manifold wisdom of God.

Christ is head of all

All of creation both in heaven and on earth is being brought into this grand sweep and everything is headed up in Christ.

We have explored this glorious theme in Ephesians and Colossians but in his letter to the Philippians also, Paul points out the supremacy of Christ:

> Therefore God exalted him to the highest place and gave him the name that is above every name, that at the name of Jesus every knee should bow, in heaven and on earth and under the earth, and every tongue confess that Jesus Christ is Lord, to the glory of God the Father. (Philippians 2:9-11)

In these passages in Ephesians, Philippians and Colossians, the scope of Christ's dominion extends to all of Creation. He is placed above everything for the church which is His body – a church where there is neither Jew nor Gentile, where believers of all nations and backgrounds are welcomed as joint members with the Lord Jesus Christ as the head.

This is the pinnacle of God's revelation of His purposes and it had been in His mind since before creation (Ephesians 1:4).

God has a mighty purpose that covers the entire cosmos. He has worked it out from the beginning of time and will bring it to conclusion when He heads up everything in Christ. However, He has revealed it progressively, calling out Abraham and choosing to bless the world through his seed. And one day that will happen, when His Spirit writes His laws on the hearts of His ancient people under the terms of the new covenant.

However, today He has a wider purpose - to bring all of creation into blessing and reconciliation by creating a body of believers, where Jews and non-Jews have equal status. This body of believers will be blessed, not on the earth like the seed of Abraham, but in the heavenly realms, where Christ is seated. By this church, God will demonstrate His manifold wisdom to all created beings in heaven, in earth and under the earth, as well as to the rulers and authorities who are located in the heavenly realms (Ephesians 3:10). This body of believers is brought to complete fullness of maturity in Christ, in whom all the fullness of deity lives. And through Christ, all creation will be reconciled to God in the dispensation of the fullness of times.

Chapter 9

In summary ...

God's unfolding purpose in the Old Testament

From the opening verses of Genesis 12 to the end of the Old Testament, the Scriptures reveal God's purposes for Abraham and his seed. Abraham was given a threefold promise as part of his covenant relationship with God:

- That he would be given a land;
- That he would become a great nation;
- That his seed would be blessed by the Lord and also be a means of blessing to the other nations on the earth.

Throughout his life, Abraham's faith was tested. To what extent was he prepared to trust in the Lord and his promises? Following the ultimate test – his willingness to sacrifice the child of promise at the Lord's command – we read:

> "I swear by myself," declares the Lord, "that because you have done this and have not withheld your son, your only son, I will surely bless you and make your descendants as numerous as the stars in the sky and as the sand on the seashore. Your descendants will take possession of the cities of their enemies, and through your offspring all nations on earth will be blessed, because you have obeyed me." (Genesis 22:16-18)

Yet, in his lifetime, Abraham never saw this promise fulfilled. He continued to live in a tent because, as the writer to the Hebrews tells us:

Abraham and his seed   125

He was looking forward to the city with foundations, whose architect and builder is God. (Hebrews 11:10)

But still the covenant relationship remained and the promise was repeated to Isaac and Jacob. The Lord's promise in Genesis 22 was unconditional and would certainly be fulfilled. But the timing of the fulfilment was uncertain as it depended on the obedience of Abraham's seed – the Israelites.

The remainder of the Old Testament traces the repeated failure of Israel to follow the Lord wholeheartedly. Yet the certainty of the Lord's covenant promises shone like a light through Israel's darkest times. Although He punished them repeatedly for their sins – even to the point of allowing them to go into exile, He showed His willingness to restore and bless them when they repented and turned to Him.

But how was this repeated repentance to become permanent? The covenant relationship established between the Lord and Abraham did not appear to have provided sufficient motivation to Abraham's seed for them to follow the Lord's ways. Even the more detailed blueprint for a godly nation, set out in the Mosaic covenant, proved no better at encouraging them to follow the Lord wholeheartedly.

Subsequently the Lord made a covenant with David that one of his descendants would sit on his throne and establish a kingdom that would last forever. In fact, if David's successors followed the Lord, all the covenant promises could have been fulfilled very quickly. Unfortunately, David's successors, like the nation as a whole, did not follow the Lord faithfully. Even Solomon, who started so well, turned away to worship other gods.

So how were the seed of Abraham to be brought to the position where they could receive the full outpouring of the Lord's promised blessings?

Jeremiah and other prophets were given a vision of a "new covenant," that the Lord would make with the house of Israel and the house of Judah. The distinguishing characteristic of this new covenant was that:

> "I will put my law in their minds and write it on their hearts. I will be their God and they will be my people. No longer will a man teach his neighbour, or a man his brother, saying, 'Know the Lord,' because they will all know me, from the least of them to the greatest," declares the Lord. "For I will forgive their wickedness and will remember their sins no more." (Jeremiah 31:33-34)

This, then, is the means by which the promises to Abraham and his seed will be fulfilled. By the end of the Old Testament, the nation were back in their land, worship of the Lord had been restored but, as Malachi observed, their service was half-hearted and their faith nominal.

How was this situation to change? 400 years after Malachi wrote, the Lord stepped into history in an extraordinary way – by sending His Son to the nation. Would His coming enable the new covenant to be implemented at last?

The coming of Jesus

The Lord Jesus came to the nation of Israel – the seed of Abraham. They were waiting for their Messiah – the One who would take the throne of His father David and restore the kingdom to Israel. And the Lord Jesus was that One. At His birth, the wise men came from the east to find "the one who has been born king of the Jews" (Matthew 2:2). He came to a nation proud of its pedigree as the seed of Abraham, yet they did not recognise Him. As John said in the opening chapter of his Gospel:

> He was in the world, and though the world was made through him, the world did not recognise him. He came to that which was his own, but his own did not receive him. (John 1:10-11)

However, in His discussions with the Jewish leaders, the Lord pointed out His connections with Abraham. He also, shockingly for them, told them that they were not, in fact, the true seed of Abraham:

> "If you were Abraham's children," said Jesus, "then you would do the things Abraham did. As it is, you are determined to kill me, a man who has told you the truth that I heard from God. Abraham did not do such things… Your father Abraham rejoiced at the thought of seeing my day; he saw it and was glad." (John 8:39-40, 56)

The Lord revealed to the Jews that they, by their rejection of Him, showed that they were not children of Abraham in spite of their physical link, but children of the devil (John 8:44).

So here, for the first time, is a suggestion that not all the natural seed of Abraham were considered by God to be true children of Abraham – only those who believed in the Lord Jesus.

At the last supper, the Lord gathered His disciples around Him to celebrate the Passover meal – a meal full of significance for the people of Israel, as they remembered their deliverance from Egypt. The Lord Jesus changed the nature of this celebration by declaring as He took the cup:

> "This cup is the new covenant in my blood, which is poured out for you." (Luke 22:20)

The Lord thus saw His sacrifice and His blood poured out as the sign of the potential implementation of the new covenant spoken of by Jeremiah. The Lord Jesus came as the heir to David's throne, who would set up the kingdom of heaven on the earth, and also, as the sacrifice for the sins of the people, enabling the new covenant to come into force.

But one of the key features of the new covenant was the writing of God's law on the hearts of the seed of Abraham. How was this to happen?

The Acts of the Apostles

In the opening chapter of Acts, we read that the risen Lord taught the disciples over a period of 40 days. He concluded this teaching by instructing them to remain in Jerusalem until they received the gift of the Holy Spirit. Their immediate response, however, was to ask:

> "Lord, are you at this time going to restore the kingdom to Israel?" (Acts 1:6)

Here we see a clear continuation of the Lord's message concerning the kingdom (e.g. Matthew 4:17; 10:7). Under the new covenant the Laws of God would be written on the hearts of the people of Israel by the work of the Holy Spirit and the disciples anticipated the Lord Jesus taking His place on David's throne.

Throughout Acts, and the epistles written at that time, the emphasis is very much on the primacy of Israel (see, for example, Romans 1:16; 2:9-10; 3:1,2). However, as Acts progresses, we find increasingly that the message was being taken to Gentiles. Initially this was limited to those who were "God-fearers" and connected to the synagogues and the religious system of Israel, but ultimately Paul and others preached the message of the risen Lord to pagans who had no connections with Israel at all.

However, this did not mean that God had abandoned the seed of Abraham. In the Galatian and Roman letters, Paul explains something of the process that was going on. The Lord Jesus had said that not all the natural descendants of Abraham were the "true" seed of Abraham – only those who believed in Him. In Galatians 3 Paul went further and argued that people who were *not* Abraham's natural descendants were included in "Abraham's seed." Paul concludes in Galatians 3:29 that:

> If you belong to Christ, then you are Abraham's seed and heirs according to the promise.

In Romans 11 Paul explained in more detail the purpose of God at that time, with his metaphor of the olive tree. Gentile "wild olive branches" were being grafted into the olive tree of Israel in the hope of stimulating the nation to respond.

> Salvation has come to the Gentiles to make Israel envious... Inasmuch as I am the apostle to the Gentiles, I make much of my ministry in the hope that I may somehow arouse my own people to envy and save some of them.
> (Romans 11:11,13-14)

During the Acts Period, God was bringing Gentiles into Abraham's seed in order to arouse the natural seed of Abraham to envy. But the ultimate hope was still the salvation of Israel. Paul sums up his argument in Romans 11 by referring again to the hope of Israel's salvation and the implementation of the covenant that will redeem the nation:

> Israel has experienced a hardening in part until the full number of the Gentiles has come in. And so all Israel will be saved, as it is written: "The deliverer will come from Zion; he will turn godlessness away from Jacob. And this is my covenant with them when I take away their sins." (Romans 11:25-27)

However, in the final chapter of Acts, when the Jewish leaders in Rome failed to be persuaded that Jesus was Israel's Messiah, Paul made a final statement, invoking Isaiah's great judgment on the nation of Israel for their hardness of heart. He declared:

> "Therefore I want you to know that God's salvation has been sent to the Gentiles and they will listen!" (Acts 28:28)

It is a moot point whether Paul understood the full implications of these words as he said them, but in the epistles written after that time we find Paul revealing a new "mystery" which had been hidden from all previous generations.

The post Acts 28 epistles

The background underpinning the vast majority of Scripture – from Genesis 12 to Acts 28 – concerns the preparation of the seed of Abraham for their role as recipients of God's blessing and for them being a means of blessing to the other nations on earth. Their destiny is to be a kingdom of priests through whom the Lord's favour to mankind will be channelled.

It is therefore important to see from the table on page 105 (Occurrences of words relating to Abraham in Paul's writings) that after Acts 28 not only are there no references to Abraham, Isaac and Jacob, but there are minimal references to Israel, Jew, circumcision and related terms. However, we should note also that those minimal references comment on the *historic* Israel or Moses, and on the *abolition* of circumcision. This, on its own, indicates a shift in emphasis.

However, the case for a change is strengthened further when we consider the language that Paul uses: he speaks of a mystery that has been hidden from all ages past, which, if understood by his readers, will enable them to have greater understanding of aspects of the "mystery of Christ." This latter mystery *had* been revealed in previous generations, but not in the way Paul was now revealing it as a result of the insight given to him by the Lord.

Christ had been revealed throughout the Old Testament. When the risen Lord walked with the two disciples on the road to Emmaus, He opened up their minds and hearts to understand this.

> Beginning with Moses and all the Prophets, he explained to them what was said in all the Scriptures concerning himself.
> (Luke 24:27)

The new dimension that was being revealed in Ephesians was the truth concerning the Lord Jesus' headship over a group of believers who would together constitute the "Body of Christ." Within the church which is His body, no one nation has priority. Gentile believers were not being brought into a group that was, essentially, Israel – the seed of Abraham. Instead all people (Jews or Gentiles) were included on the basis of their personal relationship with the Head – the Lord Jesus Christ.

The hope of the body of Christ will be realised in the heavenly realms, where Christ is seated, rather than on the new earth, which is the destiny of the seed of Abraham. Indeed, Paul states that the Lord's purpose in revealing the truth concerning the body of Christ was to reveal His manifold wisdom to the rulers and authorities in the heavenly realms, through the church (Ephesians 3:10).

As we read Paul's epistles written after Acts 28 we have a sense of everything being brought together in a state of final completeness or "fullness." Paul said that it was given to him to present the Word of God in its fullness and, in doing so, he showed the Lord Jesus Christ as possessing the fullness of God and the church as being the fullness of Christ. He also looked forward to the time when everything will be headed up in Christ in the dispensation of the fullness of times (Ephesians 1:10).

A future for the seed of Abraham?

All Christians today are members of the Body of Christ, whatever their nationality, so what will happen in the future to the seed of Abraham? Have the promises made to Abraham and his descendants been superseded by later revelation? The unconditional nature of the covenant made with Abraham and his seed and the promise of the new covenant ratified by the blood of Christ would suggest that this is not the case.
In Acts 28:26-27 Paul quoted Isaiah 6:9-10 to the Jewish leaders at Rome, condemning Israel for their unbelief and pronouncing God's judgment on them. However, if we refer back to Isaiah 6, following the judgments pronounced in verses 9-10, we read the following in verses 11-13:

Then I [Isaiah] said, '*For how long*, Lord?' And he answered:

> '*Until* the cities lie ruined
>   and without inhabitant,
> *until* the houses are left deserted
>   and the fields ruined and ravaged,
> *until* the Lord has sent everyone far away
>   and the land is utterly forsaken.
> And though a tenth remains in the land,
>   it will again be laid waste.
> But as the terebinth and oak
>   leave stumps when they are cut down,
>   so the holy seed will be the stump in the land.'

After being given the words of judgment, Isaiah's initial concern was for 'how long' the judgment would last, and the three-fold use of the word 'until' emphasises that the judgment would not be permanent. Similarly at the end of Acts: we should not think that Israel's demise at that time was to be permanent; sometime in the future they will again, as a nation, have the central place in God's purposes, and the promises made to Abraham and his seed will be fulfilled.

More on Isaiah Six

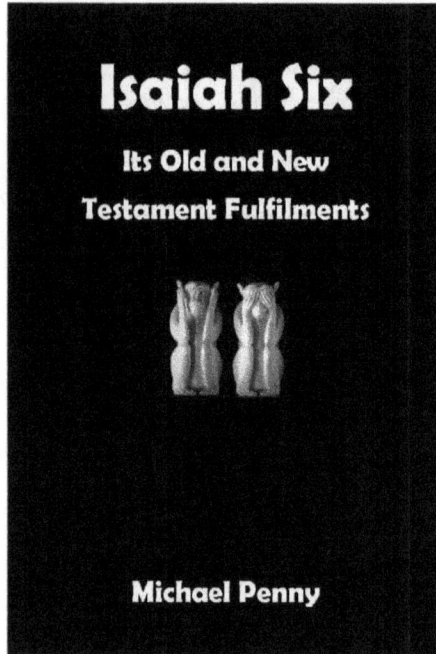

Isaiah Six

Its Old and New Testament Fulfilments

Michael Penny

Isaiah 6 is one of the most quoted Old Testament prophecies in the New Testament. An appreciation of it greatly enhances a better understanding of various parts of the New Testament.

Further details can be seen on **www.obt.org.uk**

This book be ordered from that website.

It is available as an eBook from Amazon and Apple and also as KDP paperbacks from Amazon

Appendix: A singular or a plural seed?

Galatians 3:16

There is one verse in Galatians which refers to Abraham's seed, which has not been discussed in our study. We have decided to consider it separately in an appendix because it is difficult to understand and, on the face of it, appears to contradict much of what the Scriptures have to say about the destiny of Abraham's descendants. In Galatians 3:16, Paul writes:

> The promises were spoken to Abraham and to his seed. The Scripture does not say 'and to seeds', meaning many people, but 'and to your seed', meaning one person, who is Christ.

Is Paul saying that all the promises made concerning the people of Israel – the 'literal' seed of Abraham, belong to Christ? Is he arguing that the Jews cannot expect any fulfilment of those promises made to the Fathers because they will all be fulfilled in the person of Christ? If that is what he is arguing, then he is flying in the face of much of the Old, and, indeed, the New Testament.

The Greek word for 'seed' *sperma*, (and the Hebrew *zera*) is a collective noun and can be used in both a singular and a plural sense, just as we do in English. In fact, Paul uses it in a plural sense later in Galatians 3 when he says:

> If you belong to Christ, then you are Abraham's seed, and heirs according to the promise. (Galatians 3:29)

One problem with Galatians 3:16 is that it is not clear which Scripture Paul has in mind. The footnotes in the *NIV* list three verses from the Old Testament. They are:

1. The Lord appeared to Abram and said, "To your **offspring [seed]** I will give this land." (Genesis 12:7)

2. "All the land that you see I will give to you and your **offspring [seed]** for ever." (Genesis 13:15)

3. "The Lord, the God of heaven, who brought me out of my father's household and my native land and who spoke to me and promised me on oath, saying, 'To your **offspring [seed]** I will give this land'– he will send his angel before you so that you can get a wife for my son from there." (Genesis 24:7)

However, in all three passages the context makes it clear that the 'seed' referred to is plural. These verses relate to the promise of the land, which was given to the nation of Israel, not reserved to be given to the Lord Jesus alone.

There is one other passage which may be relevant to Galatians 3:16. In Genesis 22, after Abraham showed his faith by his willingness to sacrifice Isaac, the Lord repeated the promises to him:

> I will surely bless you and make your *descendants* as numerous as the stars in the sky and as the sand on the seashore. Your *descendants* will take possession of the cities of their enemies, and through your *offspring* all nations on earth will be blessed, because you have obeyed me. (Genesis 22:17-18)

It has been suggested that the word *offspring* in verse 18 relates to Christ, whereas the word *descendants* relates to the Israelites. This is unlikely because:

1. In the Hebrew, the two occurrences of 'descendants' (verse 17) and the one occurrence of "offspring" (verse 18) is the same word, *zera*;

2. In the Septuagint (the Greek translation of the Old Testament) the same word *sperma* is used for 'descendants' in verse 17 and 'offspring' in verse 18.

The NIV rather confuses things by changing the word in English. So if the writer of Genesis was trying to say that Abraham's descendants (plural) would inherit the land but all nations would be blessed through Abraham's descendant (singular), this would mean that the same word *zera* was being used in both a singular and a plural sense in the same sentence. This interpretation therefore would require a very unnatural reading of verse 18.

So what point is Paul trying to make? Leon Morris, in a footnote in his commentary on Galatians says:

> There is evidence that some Rabbis based arguments on the use of the singular or plural of nouns in Scripture. Paul is employing a method that would have been familiar to his fellow-countrymen. (Leon Morris, *Galatians: Paul's Charter of Christian Freedom*, p110)

Morris explains:

> While his (Paul's) method may have rabbinic justification, his interpretation of the passage he quotes is most unusual even if he is drawing attention to an important scriptural truth. The term *seed* not uncommonly denotes all the descendants of some great ancestor, but it is not normally used of one person. Used in this way it points to the person as in some way outstanding; the *seed* is not simply one descendant among many, but THE descendant... It is concerned with the fact that God's chosen one,

the Christ, appeared in due course and that the covenant God made centres on him. (Morris, *ibid*, p110)

Paul wrote Galatians after his first missionary journey, when he was in Antioch in Syria (Acts 14:28). Romans was written several years later, on his third missionary journey when he was in Corinth (Acts 20:2-3). As we have seen in Romans, and in the latter part of Acts, the literal seed of Abraham still held a prominent place in God's plan and Paul was still hoping for the promises made to Abraham, Isaac and Jacob to be fulfilled.

> "And now it is because of my hope in what God has *promised our fathers* that I am on trial today. This is the *promise* our *twelve tribes* are hoping to see fulfilled as they earnestly serve God day and night." (Acts 26:6-7)

Israel's full blessings will come into force through the implementation of the new covenant. Under the new covenant, God will write His laws on the hearts of the people by His Spirit. The Lord Jesus' blood, shed on the cross is the sacrifice which will enable the new covenant to become a reality. He is the One (the seed singular) who will bring Abraham's descendants (the seed plural) to the place where they will enter into blessing. When He celebrated the last supper with His disciples, we read that:

> After taking the cup, he gave thanks and said, "Take this and divide it among you. For I tell you I will not drink again of the fruit of the vine until the kingdom of God comes"... after the supper He took the cup, saying, "This cup is the new covenant in my blood, which is poured out for you." (Luke 22:17-18, 20)

The Lord Jesus therefore links the new covenant in His blood with the establishment of the kingdom of God upon this earth. He is therefore the key to the fulfilment of the promises made to Abraham and this appears to be the message that Paul is trying to get across in Galatians 3:16.

More on the New Covenant

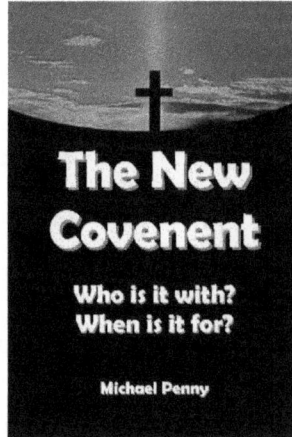

The New Covenant
By J Eustace Mills

The New Covenant
Who is it with? When is it for?
By Michael Penny

Further details can be seen on **www.obt.org.uk**

They can be ordered from that website.

They are available as eBooks from Amazon and Apple
And also as KDP paperbacks from Amazon

Index of Scripture References

Genesis

2:24	13
11:27-32	9
11:30	22
12:1	13
12:1-3	22
12:2	13
12:3	61
12:5	23
12:7	136
12:13	13
12:15	15
13:7-10	13
13:14-17	24
13:15	136
13:18	24
14:8-12	12
14:13	11
14:15-16	12
14:18-20	14
14:21	13
14:22	14
15:2	14
15:3	10
15:4	13
15:6	25,85
15:8	25
16:1-4	13
16:2	11
17:1	15,27
17:2	13,15
17:3	28
17:5	13
17:9	28
17:9-11	28,29
17:14	28
17:15-18	14
17:17	15,30
17:19	29,30
17:22	27
18:2	31
18:3-4	31
18:9-12	14
18:10	31
18:12	31
18:19	11
18:23-25	12
20:1-2	15
20:2	13
20:7	18
21:6	33
21:9-11	12
21:10	33
21:13	34
21:27	11
21:32	11
22:2	15,34
22:3-4	16
22:12	35
22:16-18	35,125
22:17-18	136,137
24:7	136
26:3-5	39
28:13-14	39

Exodus

2:24	41
3:15	41
6:2-5	41
32:13	42

Leviticus

26:40-44	42

Deuteronomy

1:8	42
6:10,12	43
10:16	58
29:5	15
29:12-13	43
30:6	58

Joshua

24:2-3	10

Judges

9:8	96

2 Samuel

7:16	115

1 Kings

6:23	96
18:36	44

2 Kings

13:22-23	44

1 Chronicles

Subject Index

Index of books quoted or referred to

Index of Hebrew and Greek words

Also on Abraham

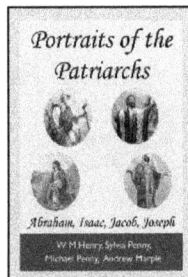

Abraham	Abraham's Progress In the Covenants of God	By Faith Abraham	Portraits of the Patriarchs
James Poole	Glen Burch	W M Henry	Abraham, Isaac, Jacob, Joseph / W M Henry, Sylvia Penny, Michael Penny, Andrew Marple

Abraham
By James Poole

Abraham's Progress in the Covenants of God
By Glen Burch

By Faith Abraham
By W M Henry

Portraits of the Patriarchs
(Abraham, Isaac, Jacob & Joseph)
By W M Henry, Andrew Marple, Michael Penny * Sylvia Penny

Further details can be seen on **www.obt.org.uk**

They can be ordered from that website.

They are available as eBooks from Amazon and Apple
And also as KDP paperbacks from Amazon

Further reading

Books by

William Henry, Michael Penny and Sylvia Penny

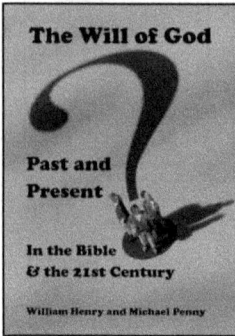

The Will of God

Past and Present

In the Bible & the 21st Century

William Henry and Michael Penny

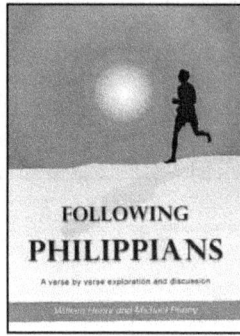

FOLLOWING

PHILIPPIANS

A verse by verse exploration and discussion

William Henry and Michael Penny

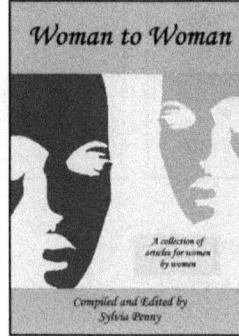

Woman to Woman

A collection of articles for women by women

Compiled and Edited by Sylvia Penny

The Will of God: Past and Present
In the Bible and in the 21st Century
By William Henry and Michael Penny

Following Philippians
A verse by verse exploration and discussion
By William Henry and Michael Penny

Woman to Woman
A collection of articles by women for women
Compiled and edited by Sylvia Penny

Further details can be seen on **www.obt.org.uk**

They can be ordered from that website.

They are available as eBooks from Amazon and Apple
And also as KDP paperbacks from Amazon

Abraham and his seed   148

www.ingramcontent.com/pod-product-compliance
Lightning Source LLC
Chambersburg PA
CBHW071546040426
42452CB00008B/1097